# WRITTEN SKILLS FOR

## QUESTIONS & ANSWERS IN

# PROPERTY PRACTICE

Hayley Mynard-Gates

Series editors: Amy and David Sixsmith

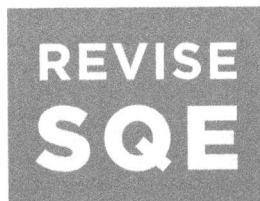

**REVISE SQE**

First published in 2024 by Fink Publishing Ltd

Impression number 10 9 8 7 6 5 4

*British Library Cataloguing in Publication Data*
A catalogue record for this book is available from the British Library
ISBN: 9781914213946

This book is also available in various ebook formats.
Ebook ISBN: 9781914213953

Cover and text design by BMLD (bmld.uk)
Production and typesetting by Westchester Publishing Services UK
Development editing by Llinos Edwards

**Fink Publishing Ltd**
**E-mail: hello@revise4law.co.uk**
**www.revise4law.co.uk**

## Acknowledgements
The author and publisher would like to thank the following copyright holders for their kind permission to reproduce material in this book:
RELX (UK) Limited, trading as LexisNexis: p. 28, extract from *Raineri v Miles and another; (Wiejski and another, third parties)* [1980] 2 All ER 145.
The Law Society: pp. 78, 83, 88, 94 Contract incorporating the Standard Conditions of Sale (Fifth Edition – 2018 revision).
We thank RELX (UK) Limited, trading as Elsevier for granting permission to reprint on p. 26: *McMeekin and another v Long and another* [2003] 2 EGLR 81 © 2003 Routledge.
Extracts from the SRA website in this book are owned by and published under licence from the Solicitors Regulation Authority of The Cube, 199 Wharfside Street, Birmingham, B1 1RN, which asserts its right to be identified as the author of this work in accordance with the Copyright, Designs and Patents Act 1988 Sections 77 and 78: www.sra.org.uk/solicitors/standards-regulations/financial-services-conduct-business-rules/. Please refer to the SRA website to ensure you are relying upon the correct version and most up to date version of the Standards.
Every effort has been made to obtain necessary permission with reference to copyright material. The publishers apologise if inadvertently any sources remain unacknowledged and will gladly make suitable arrangements with any copyright holders whom it has not been possible to contact.

## Notes from the publisher
1. While Fink Publishing has made every attempt to ensure that advice on the qualification and its assessment is accurate, the official specification and associated assessment guidance materials are the only authoritative source of information and should always be referred to for definitive guidance. See the SRA website at https://sqe.sra.org.uk. Note that the SRA may amend their assessment guidance (including the contents of the assessment specifications) at any point.
2. Fink Publishing has robust editorial processes to ensure the accuracy of the content in this publication, and every effort is made to ensure this publication is free of errors. We are, however, only human, and occasionally errors do occur. Fink Publishing is not liable for any misunderstandings that arise as a result of errors in this publication, but it is our priority to ensure that the content is accurate. If you spot an error, please do contact us at **revise4law. co.uk** so we can make sure it is corrected.

# Contents

# Contributors

## THE AUTHOR

Hayley Mynard-Gates is a qualified solicitor in England and Wales (non-practising), senior lecturer in law and associate course director on the LLB programme at Birmingham City University. She has taught property law and practice for eight years on the Legal Practice Course alongside personal injury and clinical negligence. She has previously taught land law and tort law at undergraduate level. Hayley has a plethora of experience from practising in both personal injury and property law in London firms. She was nominated for law teacher of the year 2023 with Oxford University Press and is a fellow of Advance HE. She is currently part of a team developing an SQE preparation course at Birmingham City University.

## SERIES EDITORS

Dr Amy Sixsmith is associate professor in law at the University of Sunderland and a senior fellow of Advance HE.

Dr David Sixsmith is assistant professor at Northumbria Law School and a senior fellow of Advance HE.

# Introduction

Welcome to *Revise SQE: Legal Skills for SQE2*! This series of revision guides is designed to guide you through the second element of your Solicitors Qualifying Examination, in which you will be tested on your ability to put the legal knowledge you acquired for your SQE1 assessment into six different practical contexts.

The key to successfully navigating your SQE2 assessment can be split into three distinct areas:
• understanding how you are being assessed and what you are being assessed on
• practising example scenarios
• comparing and contrasting your answers with sample answers.

Our SQE2 guides are here to help you with this process, providing you not only with helpful guidance and top tips for approaching all of the relevant skills, but also with multiple sample questions for each assessable skill in each of the relevant legal disciplines. Samples of high and lower scoring threshold answers to each question are provided, to guide you in good practice and steer you away from potential pitfalls.

Using this series in conjunction with our series of SQE1 revision guides for SQE1 to ensure that your legal knowledge is accurate and up to date, will enable you to tackle your SQE2 assessment with confidence.

## PREPARING YOURSELF FOR SQE

The SQE is the route to qualification for aspiring solicitors and consists of two parts, as shown in this table.

| Assessment | Contents of assessment |
|---|---|
| SQE1 | • 360 multiple-choice questions<br>• Closed book<br>• Assessed over 2 sittings<br>• Over 10 hours in total |
| SQE2 | • Practical legal skills<br>• 16 written and oral assessments<br>• Assesses 6 practical legal skills<br>• Over 14 hours in total |

In addition to the above assessments, all candidates will have to undertake two years' qualifying work experience. More information on the SQE assessments can be found on the SRA website.

It is important to note that the SQE can be perceived to be a 'harder' set of assessments than the Legal Practice Course (LPC). The reason for this, explained by the SRA, is that the LPC is designed to prepare candidates for 'day one' of their training contract; the SQE, on the other hand, is designed to prepare candidates for 'day one' of being a newly qualified solicitor. With that in mind, and a different style of assessments in place, it is understandable that you might feel nervous or wary of the SQE.

This revision guide series will focus on preparation for SQE2. The SQE2 assessment is challenging as it asks candidates to put into practice the knowledge that they acquired for SQE1. This style of assessment is likely to be different from what you will have experienced before. In this Introduction and revision guide series, we hope to alleviate some of those concerns, with guidance on preparing for the SQE assessment, tips on how to approach the skills-based assessments and detailed commentaries on sample answers to aid your revision.

## WHAT DOES SQE2 ENTAIL?

SQE2 is split into two parts: oral and written. The table below shows the contexts in which these skills are assessed.

| Part | Skills | Contexts |
|---|---|---|
| Oral | Client interview and attendance note / legal analysis (hereafter referred to as 'Interviewing') | Property practice<br>Wills and intestacy, probate administration and practice |
| | Advocacy | Dispute resolution<br>Criminal litigation |
| Written | Case and matter analysis<br>Legal research<br>Legal writing<br>Legal drafting | Criminal litigation<br>Dispute resolution<br>Property practice<br>Wills and intestacy, probate administration and practice<br>Business organisations, rules and procedures |

### Oral skills

You will sit four oral skills examinations, which will take place over two half-days.

On day one you will be assessed in:
• advocacy in the context of dispute resolution
• interviewing in the context of property practice.

On day two you will be assessed in:
• advocacy in the context of criminal litigation
• interviewing in the context of wills and intestacy, probate administration and practice.

### Written skills

For the written skills assessment, you will sit 12 examinations which will take place over three half-days. Every day you will be required to take an assessment in *each* of the written skills – legal research, case and matter analysis, legal writing and legal drafting.

On day one you will sit:
- two assessments in dispute resolution
- two assessments in criminal litigation.

On day two you will sit:
- two assessments in property practice
- two assessments in wills and intestacy, probate administration and practice.

On day three you will sit all four assessments in business organisations, rules and procedures.

## HOW IS SQE2 MARKED?

Each of the SQE2 skills has its own set of assessment criteria. The *Revise SQE: Legal Skills for SQE2* series will include the following:
- Oral skills – the criteria are outlined in *Oral Skills for SQE2: Client Interviewing and Negotiation* and *Oral Skills for SQE2: Advocacy*.
- Written skills – the criteria are outlined at the beginning of each chapter in our books covering the written skills for different legal contexts (see pages 2, 20, 56 and 75 in this text).

The assessment is marked against the relevant criteria using the following scale:
A. Superior performance: well above the competency requirements of the assessment.
B. Clearly satisfactory: clearly meets the competency requirements of the assessment.
C. Marginal pass: on balance, just meets the competency requirements of the assessment.
D. Marginal fail: on balance, just fails to meet the competency requirements of the assessment.
E. Clearly unsatisfactory: clearly does not meet the competency requirements of the assessment.
F. Poor performance: well below the competency requirements of the assessment.

Your mark will be calculated by converting the grade into a numerical mark, with A representing 5 marks and F representing 0 marks.

### The scaled scoring system

In January 2025 the SRA introduced a scaled scoring system for all SQE2 assessments. This approach is designed to ensure that candidate scores are comparable across different assessment sittings, thereby providing a fair and consistent measure of candidate performance. The same system has already been implemented for all SQE1 assessments.

The scaled scoring system works in the following way:
- Initially, candidates will receive a 'raw score' based on their performance across the 16 assessment stations in SQE2.
- A pass mark is then set for each assessment window. The pass mark is determined using statistical methods that account for any differences in question difficulty. This ensures fairness across different exam versions.
- Candidate raw scores are then converted to a common scale ranging from 0 to 500, with the pass mark consistently set at 300. This standardisation allows for direct comparisons between candidates' performances, regardless of the specific assessments they completed.

When you access your results, you will be able to see:

- a detailed breakdown of your results by assessment station (results will be expressed as marks from 0 to 5 for each assessment criterion across each of the 16 assessment stations)
- your overall mark expressed as a percentage
- your scaled score out of 500 – remember that the pass mark will always be set at 300.

For more information about the scaled scoring system, visit https://sqe.sra.org.uk/SQEHomePage.

It is very important that you are aware of the standard you are required to meet. The competence standard is that of a Day One Solicitor, which is mapped against Level 3 of the Threshold Standard for the Statement of Solicitor Competence. This is available on the SRA website, and we would encourage you to review this prior to sitting your SQE2 assessment.

### The assessors

In terms of who will be assessing you against this standard and the relevant skills criteria, the interview will be marked by the person you are interviewing, while the remaining assessments (attendance note, advocacy and all written skills) will be marked by a solicitor. All assessors will have received training on how to assess a candidate's performance against the relevant criteria. It is therefore essential that you tackle your assessments in the same way that you would if you were a fully qualified solicitor on the first day of practice, ie with professionalism, confidence and calmness. This will come across to the assessors in the examination itself: remember that they are fundamentally assessing your suitability for practice!

## WHERE DOES *REVISE SQE* COME INTO IT?

This new series of revision guides for SQE2 will provide you with helpful tips and advice on how to tackle each skill assessment in the relevant contexts. Each book provides a range of example threshold answers to SQE2-style assessment questions, which you can use to practise and assess your answers against, to see how you are performing in each individual area. This is designed to assist with your revision and consolidate your understanding of how key topics could be assessed in the SQE2 examinations. We hope that this series will give clarity for assessment focus, provide useful tips for sitting SQE2 and act as a general revision aid.

Finally, always keep in mind that while SQE2 is primarily a skills-based assessment, you are still being tested on your knowledge of the law. It is therefore important that you conduct an honest self-evaluation on the areas of the SQE1 specification with which you feel you need further support.*Revise SQE* can help you with this:

- Check out the 'SQE1 Revision Checklist' for each of our SQE1 revision guides on our website: **www.revise4law.co.uk**. These will help you to identify which substantive topics you feel confident about being assessed on, and which ones you need to revise.
- All of our *Revise SQE* revision guides are mapped to the relevant SRA specifications for SQE1. Before taking the SQE2 assessments, remember to look back at our revision guides for SQE1 if you have any gaps in your legal knowledge.

# Case and matter analysis

## ■ MAKE SURE YOU KNOW

This chapter looks at case and matter analysis in the context of property law. This is one of the legal skills that may be assessed on day one of the SQE2 assessments (see the Introduction for more detail). When assessing this skill, the SQE2 will test candidates' ability to analyse and apply the law to a client's situation alongside demonstrating an understanding of what a client wants to achieve. Candidates are expected to apply knowledge in both property and land law to these scenarios. It is therefore necessary to read this revision guide in addition to the contents of **Revise SQE: Land Law** and **Revise SQE: Property Practice**. Enforcement of planning law and leases are developed further within this chapter to identify the ways in which SQE2 skills assessments incorporate the legal principles you will have learned for your SQE1 examinations.

This chapter provides examples of what options are available in relation to the enforcement of planning law and commercial leases. It identifies the potential options available to clients, in addition to providing client-focused advice to achieve the outcomes that the client wants, which could arise in the context of a case and matter analysis SQE2 assessment.

## ■ SQE ASSESSMENT ADVICE

As you work through this chapter, pay attention in your revision to:
- the documents provided to you to assist in the analysis task in the sample answers
- the structure used in the letter of advice for ease of use by the reader
- the way in which the letter of advice is tailored to the recipient
- addressing all relevant legal and factual issues
- using clear, precise, concise and acceptable language
- ensuring the law is applied correctly to the client's situation
- the way in which any ethical or professional conduct issues are identified and resolved.

See the Appendix for the SRA's performance indicators in case and matter analysis.

## ■ INTRODUCTION TO CASE AND MATTER ANALYSIS IN PROPERTY PRACTICE

The SQE2 assessments aim to replicate scenarios from practice, reflecting day-to-day issues in the field of property law. As with all areas of law, a key aspect of practising in the field of property is the ability to clearly and accurately apply the law and identify solutions for clients. The SQE2 assessment in case and matter analysis will be to write a report for your partner, which provides legal analysis of a case in addition to client-focused advice. While the question itself will give you some direction about the areas you need to cover in your advice, you will be required to apply your knowledge of those areas to the scenario and communicate the relevant advice to your partner clearly and concisely in writing. This chapter will provide examples of how you can do this and meet the criteria for SQE2 case and matter analysis assessment at the same time.

The key to success in your SQE2 case and matter analysis assessment is approaching the question in a structured manner. Try adopting the following approach:

1. Once you have read the question, write down the key legal and procedural points that you will need to communicate to the recipient.
2. Write your answer, making sure you:
   - analyse and provide an explanation for all options available to your client, and then
   - identify the best option for client in this specific situation.
3. Review your answer, keeping in mind the SQE case and matter analysis assessment criteria (below).

## Assessment technique

When exploring the enforcement of planning law, it is useful to identify and consider all of the options that are available in a particular scenario before undertaking legal analysis. Once this has been done, you can then reach an informed decision on which the most appropriate would be, based on the client's wishes. This is to ensure that you do not miss an option that may be more appropriate for the client's circumstances. It also shows the examiners that you can demonstrate an understanding of the problem from the client's point of view, and not just from a legal perspective, in line with the SQE2 case and matter analysis assessment criteria.

## SQE2 case and matter analysis assessment criteria

Ensure that you follow these criteria when drafting your answer:

### Skills

1. Identify relevant facts.
2. Provide client-focused advice (ie advice which demonstrates an understanding of the problem from the client's point of view and what the client wants to achieve, not just from a legal perspective).
3. Use clear, precise, concise and acceptable language.

### Application of law

4. Apply the law correctly to the client's situation.
5. Apply the law comprehensively to the client's situation, identifying any ethical and professional conduct issues and exercising judgement to resolve them honestly and with integrity.

In chapter 3 of *Revise SQE: Property Practice*, we considered core principles and enforcement of planning matters. Question 1 below demonstrates how your knowledge of this topic could be assessed in the context and format of an SQE2 case and matter analysis assessment.

# ■ QUESTION 1

## Email to candidate

**From:** Partner
**Sent:** 22 September 202#
**To:** Candidate
**Subject:** Purchase of property

I received an email yesterday from my client, Vincenzo Marchetti, who is in the process of purchasing a freehold property with a view to making some alterations to the property. He is a cash purchaser and therefore there is no lender involved in the transaction. Vincenzo advised me that he previously built a single-storey extension and conservatory in his last property without the need for planning permission. He thinks that it is because it fell under permitted development, but he cannot remember exactly, or whether he just did not obtain planning permission. The seller has been trying to sell the property for over a year and is very happy that Vincenzo is purchasing the property.

### The initial meeting
Vincenzo would like to make some alterations to the property once the property has been purchased. He would like to build a single-storey side extension and conservatory along the back of the property to create a snug area and games room. If he cannot go ahead with these additions, then he does not want to purchase the property as without this, there will not be enough room to house his pool table and arcade games.

I have attached the email from Vincenzo confirming his position (Attachment 1) and a copy of the local search result (Attachment 2).

### Important background information
As you will see from Vincenzo's email, he would like to avoid the need for planning permission and thinks that this will be possible by ensuring that these amendments fall within permitted development. However, a friend of his was recently fined for not obtaining planning permission, so Vincenzo is understandably nervous and would like to avoid any financial penalties. Vincenzo confirmed that he will be the sole occupier of the property.

### Advice and analysis required
Vincenzo would like advice about the options which are available to him. He would like to continue with the purchase and, as noted above, not have the added hassle or expense of obtaining any planning permission. He also wants to know of any risks or actions that could be taken against him if he were to continue with his plans without notifying the local authority. He does not want to have to pay more than necessary, but equally would like to avoid any penalties. He would also like suggestions to negotiate a better position for himself.

Can I please ask that you provide me with some advice and analysis in relation to Vincenzo's position, so that I can write a letter to him advising him accordingly. Please note that I will require a brief explanation of the relevant law so that I do not have to look this up. The client has advised that we do not need to look into building regulations consent as his builder will be handling this.

**Please set out your advice and analysis on the following:**

1. Based on the contents of the local authority search in Attachment 2, what are the potential risks that Vincenzo faces if he were to proceed as planned? You should consider the advantages and disadvantages of these risks. This will allow Vincenzo to be fully informed before making a final decision.
2. Considering the client's wishes, what alternative options would you suggest? You should keep in mind Vincenzo's wishes on keeping down the costs, but also bear in mind the seller and what they are likely to agree to.

Thanks

Partner

**Attachment 1**

From: Vincenzo Marchetti
To: Partner
Sent: 21 September 202#
Subject: Planning permission enquiry about my purchase

Good afternoon,

Thank you for meeting me and going through the search results.
I just wanted to mention that I really do not want to incur any further costs and would ideally like to avoid having to apply for planning permission. As such, I have looked into what changes can be made under permitted development and will only be making these alterations. Can you please confirm that this is OK? If it is not, can you please advise what can be done to keep the costs to a minimum, as I have a limited budget and do not want to have to take out a mortgage on this property. I am keen to move forward with the purchase but do not want to have to pay any more than I am already paying.

I look forward to hearing from you.

Kind regards,

Vincenzo Marchetti

**Attachment 2**

**NOTICE TO OWNERS AND OCCUPIERS IN THE NORTH FIELDS CONSERVATION AREA IN LANDCHESTER CITY COUNCIL 13 OCTOBER 2019 TOWN AND COUNTRY PLANNING (GENERAL PERMITTED DEVELOPMENT) (ENGLAND) ORDER 2015**

**CONFIRMATION OF DIRECTION MADE UNDER ARTICLE 4(1)**

WHEREAS LANDCHESTER CITY COUNCIL, being the appropriate local planning authority within the meaning of article 4(5) of the Town and Country Planning (General Permitted Development) (England) Order 2015, is satisfied that it is expedient that development of the descriptions set out in Schedule One below should not be carried out on land within the North Fields Conservation Area within Landchester City Council as shown on the deposited plans, unless permission is granted on an application made under Part III of the Town and Country Planning Act 1990 as amended.

NOW THEREFORE the said Council, in pursuance of the power conferred on them by article 4(1) of the Town and Country Planning (General Permitted Development) Order 2015, hereby CONFIRM that the permission granted by article 3 of the said order shall not apply to development on the said land of the descriptions set out in the Schedule below.

Notice of the proposed Direction was made on the 3rd May 2019. Representations relating to the Direction were invited by the Council for a period of 28 days and closed on the 31st May 2019. Notice is hereby given that the Council has considered the representation received and has determined to confirm the Direction.

**Landchester City Council (North Fields Conservation Area) article 4(1) Direction 2019.**

**Town & Country Planning (General Permitted Development) (England) Order 2015: Classes of Permitted Development CONFIRMED to be withdrawn**

**SCHEDULE ONE**
Permitted Development Rights Withdrawn

*   *   *

## ■ YOUR TURN

Have a go at answering question 1, remembering the guidance on pages 1–2.
- Refer to the structured approach in the SRA's assessment criteria on page 2.
- Create a list of the options available to the client and then analyse these to identify the best advice to provide to the client.
- Timings are important: you will need to prepare and write your answer in one hour. You will need to adhere to this time frame to ensure you adequately deal with the question in your SQE2 assessment.

| SQE1 Functioning legal knowledge link |
|---|
| Remember from chapter 3 of **Revise SQE: Property Practice** that an article 4 direction revokes general permitted development orders (GPDO). If this is shown on a local search result, planning permission will be required (even if it would usually not be under GPDO). |

## EVALUATING YOUR ANSWER

When you have attempted question 1, mark it yourself against the SQE2 case and matter analysis assessment criteria. Do you think your attempt met the threshold standard? Reflect on any improvements that you could make.

Now compare your attempt with the following key legal points and two sample answers to question 1. A circled number indicates that commentary is provided for this part of the answer. The commentary will explain whether the sample is likely to meet the threshold SQE2 standard.

---

**➡Key legal points: Question 1**

---

- You will always need to check the local search results for a property before advising a client. Even if changes proposed to the property would usually fall within permitted development rights, planning permission will still likely be required if the property is situated within a conservation area, is listed or has an article 4 direction in place.
- When a property falls within a conservation area or there is an article 4 direction in place, if planning permission is necessary and not obtained then the local authority could issue a planning contravention notice, which would require the owner of the property to respond within 21 days.
- If the local authority deems there to be a breach of planning control, they could issue a completion notice, enforcement notice, stop notice, breach of condition notice or an injunction.
- When providing clients with advice, remember to tailor the advice to their situation. If a particular notice is not relevant to the client's situation, do not discuss it in depth. This will show the examiners that you understand what is applicable in line with the SQE2 assessment criteria.

## ■ SAMPLE ANSWER 1 TO QUESTION 1

Under the Town and Country Planning (General Permitted Development) Order 2015, an extension or conservatory would usually fall within general permitted development and therefore would not require planning permission. ❶

However, under the current local authority search results, it is likely that Vincenzo will be required to obtain planning permission for the proposed alterations to the property. This is because there is an article 4 direction noted within the local authority search, which indicates that permitted development rights will likely not apply. ❷

### 1. What are the potential risks to Vincenzo?

If Vincenzo continues with the purchase and makes the relevant alterations to the property without the necessary planning permission, it is likely that the local authority will deem there to be a breach of planning control. They may take enforcement action against him, which could prove to be expensive. They could issue any of the following: ❸

- Enforcement Notice – the local authority could issue an enforcement notice on Vincenzo if they feel it is appropriate. This would identify the relevant breaches and what he would need to do to rectify this. Although Vincenzo could appeal this, ignoring the notice is a criminal offence which could result in a costly fine. ❹
- Stop Notice – this would effectively stop Vincenzo from making alterations until any appeal made has been reviewed. It can only be issued after an enforcement notice has been issued. Similar to an enforcement notice, it is a criminal offence not to comply with this. However, with stop notices, there is no right to appeal. ❺
- Injunction – this is an equitable remedy that can be sought by the local authority to stop Vincenzo from continuing with the alterations without obtaining planning permission. However, it is important to note that this is at the discretion of the court and unlikely to be issued if they deem an alternative remedy to be more appropriate. ❻

## 2.  What alternative option/s would you suggest?

It is worth discussing the above with Vincenzo and potentially negotiating with the seller for them to obtain planning permission prior to exchange of contracts. Although this may delay the transaction, it would provide Vincenzo with security so that he can make the alterations once he has purchased the property. If the planning permission is refused, he can withdraw from the transaction prior to exchange of contracts and find another property. This would ensure that he does not suffer any financial repercussions while also being able to guarantee that he can make the changes that he wants to the property. The seller may be amenable to this, given that they have been trying to sell the property for over a year and may not want to risk Vincenzo withdrawing. We should therefore start from this position. If this is not agreed by the seller, Vincenzo could contact the local authority directly to see if this would be a possibility (preferably in writing). ❼

If Vincenzo does not wish to follow either of the above suggestions, then he might wish to withdraw from the transaction before he is tied into the purchase. If he wants to continue with the purchase, he will need to be advised that he will likely require planning permission if he wants to make any alterations due to the article 4 direction, and that this is not guaranteed. In addition, if he does not obtain this, there could be severe financial repercussions from enforcement action of the local authority. ❽

## COMMENTARY

❶ The first paragraph explicitly refers to the Town and Country Planning (General Permitted Development) Order 2015 and correctly applies the facts of the alterations the client wants to make, to identify that these would usually fall within permitted development.

❷ This paragraph takes this explanation one step further and identifies that although it would usually fall under permitted development, because there is an article 4 direction in place (highlighted on the local search result) that this will likely require planning permission (as an article 4 direction revokes the general permitted development order). This is covered in **Revise SQE: Property Practice** and evidences to an examiner that the candidate is able to apply the law correctly to the client's situation.

❸ This paragraph clearly identifies that Vincenzo is at risk of being in breach of planning control if he does not obtain planning permission due to the article 4 direction. This identifies to an examiner that the candidate is able to apply the law to the client scenario in addition to understanding the need to explain the repercussions to the client. It is extremely important that clients are provided with a full picture of the risks to them so that they can make informed decisions.

❹ This paragraph concisely and precisely explains what an enforcement notice is, in addition to the steps to be taken to remedy the breach. It highlights the financial risk to the client which demonstrates to an examiner the candidate's ability to understand the client's wishes. It is therefore likely that this paragraph would meet the SQE2 case and matter analysis assessment criteria.

❺ This paragraph clearly identifies that a stop notice can only be issued once an enforcement notice has been served. It highlights to an examiner that the candidate is aware of the risks and the need to manage the clients' expectations by identifying that it is a criminal offence to contravene it, which could result in a fine – exactly what the client wanted to avoid. This evidences an understanding of the client's wishes.

❻ This paragraph shows the examiner that the candidate has taken into consideration all of the facts available in addition to the risks, and has identified that although possible, an injunction is a discretionary equitable remedy and may not be granted. This effectively evidences an ability to apply the law correctly.

❼ This paragraph identifies the need to ask the seller whether they would be willing to obtain planning permission prior to exchange of contracts. It takes into consideration the client's wishes to avoid any penalties and protects the client from assuming the alterations fall within the remit of permitted development. It shows to an examiner the ability to identify the client's concerns and find appropriate solutions to meet their needs. It also showcases an ability to interpret the facts provided and identify that this approach may be a possibility due to the seller's circumstances.

(8) Finally, this paragraph identifies alternative options for the client to take should the seller not be agreeable to obtaining planning permission before the exchange of contracts takes place. This is client-focused advice and is therefore likely to meet the SQE2 case and matter analysis assessment criteria.

## Does this answer meet the threshold?

The sample answer above effectively identifies the potential risks to the client alongside the best options available to him. It correctly identifies that although a conservatory may fall within permitted development, planning permission will still be required where there is an article 4 direction. The answer demonstrates an understanding of the problem from the client's point of view and what the client wants to achieve. It is likely to meet the threshold standard for the SQE2 case and matter analysis assessment.

Now consider the second sample answer to question 1.

## ■ SAMPLE ANSWER 2 TO QUESTION 1

The Town and Country Planning (General Permitted Development) Order 2015 is applicable in this instance. Under this order, extensions fall within general permitted development and therefore would not require planning permission. (1)

### 1. What are the potential risks to Vincenzo?

If Vincenzo's planned alterations exceed what falls within permitted development, it is likely that he will then require planning permission. Without this, he could face potential consequences from the local authority who have enforcement powers. This could prove to be expensive. There are five potential actions that the local authority could take here that would be relevant to Vincenzo's situation. They could issue a completion notice, an enforcement notice, a stop notice, a breach of condition notice or an injunction. (2)

- Completion notice – the local authority can force Vincenzo to complete the works within a specified time frame. (3)
- Enforcement or Stop notice – the local authority could issue an enforcement or stop notice on Vincenzo if they feel it is appropriate. Although Vincenzo could appeal this, ignoring it is a criminal offence which could result in a costly fine. (4)
- Breach of condition notice – this would require Vincenzo to comply with the conditions within a certain time frame. (5)
- Injunction – the local authority could stop Vincenzo from continuing with the alterations without obtaining planning permission. (6)

### 2. What alternative option/s would you suggest?

As mentioned above, providing Vincenzo adheres to alterations that fall within permitted development, there is no need for alternative options. However, if he wants to exceed the permitted development constraints, one option would be to buy the property and then apply for planning permission. However, this could be expensive, and it is worth noting that if he did not obtain planning permission and providing the local authority is unaware of the alterations for four years, they will not be able to bring enforcement action against Vincenzo. Ultimately, it is the client's decision. (7)

## COMMENTARY

**1** This paragraph does not evidence to an examiner that the candidate has fully understood the law in relation to permitted development. While some extensions may fall within permitted development, this paragraph fails to apply the law correctly to the client's situation. An article 4 direction has shown up in the local search result and therefore the client is likely to need planning permission. It is unlikely that this paragraph would meet the SQE2 case and matter analysis assessment criteria.

**2** This paragraph is incorrect as it reinforces that Vincenzo will not need planning permission unless he exceeds what he had originally planned. In addition to this, it lists all potential actions. However, some of these would not be applicable to the client's situation, as explained below. Candidates often fall into the trap of including everything, to be on the safe side. However, this does not evidence knowledge and understanding, and it therefore fails to provide client-based advice. Try to avoid doing this in the SQE2 assessments.

**3** While this information in this paragraph is correct, it is not applicable to the client's scenario. This would usually apply if he had obtained planning permission and had not adhered to the date that the works should have been implemented. This does not evidence to an examiner that the candidate is able to apply the law correctly to a client's situation as in this instance, the client has not yet obtained planning permission.

**4** This paragraph is confusing as it fails to identify that a stop notice can only be issued once an enforcement notice has been issued. This does not demonstrate an understanding of the law in relation to the client scenario as it fails to differentiate between the two. It does not explain each one and fails to identify that a stop notice cannot be appealed.

**5** While this is an enforcement power, it is not applicable to the client's circumstances. Vincenzo has not yet sought planning permission, and therefore there could not have been a breach of the conditions attached to the planning permission, as it is not yet in existence. The candidate does not apply the relevant law or provide correct client-focused advice. In addition, the answer does not mention that failure to comply with a breach of condition notice is also a criminal offence for which there is no right to appeal.

**6** While this clause is technically correct, it does not mention that this is a discretionary equitable remedy which is unlikely if there are alternative remedies available. It does not adequately manage client expectations and does not evidence a solid understanding of the law.

**7** This paragraph is incorrect and misleading towards the client. This could potentially result in a claim being made against the firm for professional negligence as it fails to advise the client that if he knowingly conceals the changes to the property, the Localism Act 2011 allows for the local planning authorities to apply to the magistrates' court to allow enforcement outside the statutory time limits.

## Does this answer meet the threshold?

It is unlikely that this written report would meet the threshold standard for the SQE2 case and matter analysis assessment. When assessed against the SQE2 case and matter analysis assessment criteria, it does not provide correct legal analysis and the advice to the client is not to an appropriate professional level. Misinformation is provided which could result in the local planning authority bringing enforcement action against the client, requiring him to put the property back to its original state. This could potentially result in significant financial repercussions on behalf of the client, in addition to a professional negligence claim being made against the firm.

Below is a different example, in relation to a lease, which could also arise in the context of case and matter analysis in SQE2.

# ■ QUESTION 2

## Email to candidate

**From:** Partner
**Sent:** 5 October 202#
**To:** Candidate
**Subject:** Alterations to lease

I received a call yesterday from a new client, Marcella Rodriguez, who is having a few problems with the property that she has been leasing for the last nine years. The original landlord was very laid-back in relation to allowing the client certain deviations with some of the provisions in the lease. These were informal arrangements, and nothing was ever put in writing. However, the original landlord sold the freehold last year and since then, the new landlord has been less accommodating.

**The initial meeting**
Marcella would like to make some internal alterations to the property, in readiness for the lease renewal which will be next year. She would like to erect internal partitions, to create a private office environment. In addition, she wants to include some signs in the window and externally to advertise to people passing by the shop. She knows that this is not permitted in the current lease. However, previously her original landlord allowed her free rein over the property. The new landlord has told Marcella that she cannot make any internal changes and has asked that she remove the signs that she has put up. Marcella is understandably upset by this as she has paid a significant sum of money for these signs. She wants to know what she can do moving forward.

After speaking to Marcella, she emailed across some further information (Attachment 1) and a copy of the lease (Attachment 2).

**Important background information**
As you will see from Marcella's email, she ideally wants to remain in the property and would like to renegotiate some of the terms of the lease. She has around 11 months left under her current lease, and she has exclusive possession of the property. The lease that she currently has is for a period of ten years and she uses the property as a shop selling laptops, computers and printers, with some office rental space booked by clients daily. Marcella confirmed that she is the sole occupier of the property.

**Advice and analysis required**
Marcella would like advice about what options are available to her. She would like to remain in the property as she has built a client base and has repeat customers. She does not want to have to start again. She would also like suggestions to negotiate a better position for herself, but must bear in mind her new landlord, as she does not want to upset him.

Can I please ask that you provide me with some advice and analysis in relation to Marcella's position, so that I can write a letter to her. Please note that I will require a brief explanation of the relevant law so that I do not have to look this up. As we are still in the preliminary stages, I do not need you to provide a redrafted lease, just consider the points mentioned in the attached documentation.

**Please set out your advice and analysis on the following:**

1. Based on the contents of the lease extract in Attachment 2, what are the options available to Marcella? You should consider the advantages and disadvantages of these. This will allow Marcella to be fully informed before making a final decision.
2. Assuming the landlord agrees to new terms of the lease, what alternative provisions would you suggest? You should suggest provisions that will benefit Marcella, but also keep in mind the landlord and what they are likely to agree to.

Thanks

Partner

**Note to candidates: Only an extract of the lease has been provided for the purposes of this question.**

### Attachment 1

From: Marcella Rodriguez
To: Partner
Sent: 1 October 202#
Subject: Lease enquiries

Good morning,

Thank you for meeting me. I have attached a copy of the lease for you to look at. I really hope you can help me.

I also wanted to mention that I really do not want to have to look elsewhere for another building for my shop. I have built up a reputation here and have quite a few local customers. I worry that if I were to move, I would lose all of these local customers and in the current climate, I am not sure that my business would be able to survive the loss of the repeat custom. Ideally, I would like to put up internal partitions to create individual office spaces and entice more businesses to use my shop.
Let me know if you need anything else.

Warmest regards,

Marcella Rodriguez

### Attachment 2

**LEASE**

**LAND REGISTRY PRESCRIBED CLAUSES**

| LR1. Date of lease | 31st January 202# |
|---|---|
| LR2. Title number(s) | WM299376 |
| LR2.1 Landlord's title number(s) | WM10976 |
| LR2.2 Other title numbers | None |
| LR3. Parties to this lease | |
| Landlord | MR ALEKSY KAMINSKI of 4 Bloomsbury Avenue, Coventry, CV1 7TF. |
| Tenant | MS MARCELLA RODRIGUEZ of 39 Hyde Lane, Castle Vale, West Midlands, B35 9YD. |

| LR4. Property | **In the case of a conflict between this clause and the remainder of this lease then, for the purposes of registration, this clause shall prevail.** The property described as the 'Property' in **clause 1** of this lease. |
|---|---|
| **LR5. Prescribed statements etc.** | None. |
| **LR6. Term for which the property is leased** | The term starting on 31st January 202# and ending on 31st January 202# (10 years). |
| **LR7. Premium** | None. |
| **LR8. Prohibitions or restrictions on disposing of this lease** | This lease contains a provision that prohibits or restricts dispositions. |
| **LR9. Rights of acquisition etc.** | |
| **LR9.1 Tenant's contractual rights to renew this lease, to acquire the reversion or another lease of the property, or to acquire an interest in other land** | None. |
| **LR9.2 Tenant's covenant to (or offer to) surrender this lease** | None. |
| **LR9.3 Landlord's contractual rights to acquire this lease** | None. |
| **LR10. Restrictive covenants given in this lease by the landlord in respect of land other than the property** | None. |
| **LR11. Easements** | |
| **LR11.1 Easements granted by this lease for the benefit of the property** | None. |
| **LR11.2 Easements granted or reserved by this lease over the property for the benefit of other property** | None. |
| **LR12. Estate rent charge burdening the property** | None. |
| **LR13. Application for standard form of restriction** | None. |
| **LR14. Declaration of trust where there is more than one person comprising the tenant** | The tenant is a single legal entity. |

**Clause 7**
**Alterations**
The tenant must not build any new structure on or alter the external appearance, or cut into any structural part of, the property.

**Clause 13**
**Signs and advertisements**
The tenant must not display any signs or advertisements on the property visible outside the property.

\*    \*    \*

## ■ YOUR TURN

Have a go at answering question 2, remembering the guidance on pages 1–2.
- Refer to the structured approach in the SRA's assessment criteria on page 2.
- Create a list of the relevant options available to the client and then analyse these to identify the best advice to be provided to your client.
- Timings are important: you will need to prepare and write your answer in one hour.

| SQE1 Functioning legal knowledge link |
| --- |
| Remember from chapter 9 of **Revise SQE: Property Practice** that a s 25 notice is a notice by the landlord to terminate a fixed-term periodic tenancy. A s 26 notice is a tenant's request to terminate an existing fixed-term tenancy. |

## EVALUATING YOUR ANSWER

When you have attempted question 2, mark it yourself against the SQE2 case and matter analysis assessment criteria. Do you think your attempt met the threshold standard?

Now compare your attempt with the following key legal points and two sample answers to question 2. A circled number indicates that commentary is provided for this part of the answer. The commentary will explain whether the sample is likely to meet the threshold SQE2 standard.

### ➥Key legal points: Question 2

- Remember the purpose of the report. If a client is asking for advice, it is important to provide all options available before identifying the most appropriate. You also need to explore the advantages and disadvantages so that the client has all the information and can make an informed decision.
- In instances where a landlord seeks to request a new tenancy, this needs to be done under a s 25 request. However, if a tenant seeks to request a new tenancy, this needs to be done under a s 26 request. It is important that this is done in a prescribed form to ensure its validity. In addition, it cannot be given less than 6 months or more than 12 months prior to the start date stated in the notice. It will also need to include the proposed new terms of the tenancy.
- In instances where a client seeks to surrender the lease to the landlord, and the landlord accepts the surrender, this must be surrendered by deed under s 52 of the Law of Property Act. If this is not done, it will not be surrendered. However, it is also important to consider the goal of the client. Where the client has a successful, established business, although a surrender may appear to be a more simple/cheaper option, it may not be what the client wants to do.

## ■ SAMPLE ANSWER 1 TO QUESTION 2

Under the current lease, Marcella cannot display any signs or advertisements, nor can she make internal alterations. If nothing is changed, this will continue until the lease is terminated. ❶

The Landlord and Tenant Act 1954 is likely to apply here as Marcella has a business tenancy. She has exclusive possession and occupies the property for business purposes (her shop), and has not contracted out of the Act to our knowledge. ❷

### 1.  What are the options available to Marcella?

Under the Landlord and Tenant Act 1954, Marcella has security of tenure. This will provide a certain level of security by providing a 'renewal lease' which will usually be similar to the previous lease. If Marcella cannot agree the terms, the court can intervene to determine it. If they decide not to grant it based on the landlord's opposition, Marcella may be entitled to compensation. However, this could become a costly exercise and there are a few alternative options available to Marcella. ❸

It may give Marcella more security if she were to serve a request for a new tenancy under s 26 of the Landlord and Tenant Act 1954 Part II. However, if it were not agreed by the landlord, the onus would be on Marcella to convince the court of the new terms. One of the downsides is that this could result in her rent increasing sooner than she anticipated. However, this would be likely within the next year anyway due to the upcoming end date of the lease. In addition, it may increase the lease's marketability if this has already been granted. ❹

If negotiations break down between Marcella and the landlord, Marcella does have the option to surrender the lease under s 52 of the Law of Property Act 1925. However, it is worth noting that this would need to be done by deed for it to be legal. What this would do is effectively merge the leasehold with the landlord's reversion and extinguish it. However, as Marcella has previously advised, she has set up her business from nothing and has built a client base with repeat customers. As she does not want to have to move and start again, this option would not be best suited for her. ❺

Although all the options set out above are available to Marcella, based on the client's wishes, it would be worth entering into negotiations with the landlord to negotiate a new tenancy with varied terms. Given that the lease is due to expire within the next year, in order to provide Marcella with the most security it would be beneficial for her to serve a notice under s 26 of the Landlord and Tenant Act 1954 Part II. This would ensure that negotiations to vary certain terms are entered into but would also provide further protection of a new lease. ❻

### 2.  What alternative provisions would you suggest?

I would suggest the following amendments to clauses 7 and 13 of the lease:

**Clause 7**
**Alterations**
7.  The tenant may, without needing consent, install demountable, non-structural partitions in the property including (where necessary) fixings to the structure of the property, but:
  **7.1**   the fixings must not adversely affect:
      **(a)** the property's structural integrity; nor
      **(b)** adjoining property; nor
      **(c)** the energy efficiency of the property or any existing EPC; and

**7.2** if the tenant does install partitions, it must promptly notify the landlord that it has done so and:

    **(a)** supply:

        **(i)** reasonable details of what it has done;

        **(ii)** a certificate from a suitably qualified person addressed to the landlord confirming compliance; and

    **(b)** insofar as CDM 2015 apply to those works, the tenant must:

        **(i)** carry out the role of 'client' pursuant to them; and

        **(ii)** indemnify the landlord against all costs arising wholly or partly, directly, or indirectly, in respect of any breach of them.

As it was originally drafted, this was an absolute covenant, which did not provide the client with any room for negotiation. If Marcella were to proceed without any changes, she could risk forfeiting the lease. However, with the proposed amendment above, the tenant will be allowed a certain amount of freedom. It will enable her to make non-structural changes to the property, without needing to seek permission from the landlord. It will also provide a level of protection to the landlord, as she would keep control in relation to structural changes, which would provide protection against the devaluation of the property. If this is not agreeable by the landlord, another suggestion could be 'The tenant may carry out internal, non-structural works only if it obtains consent, not to be unreasonably withheld'. However, this would not give Marcella so much freedom in terms of what she wants to achieve and would require permission before making any internal alterations. We should therefore start from the position above. ❼

**Clause 13**

**Signs and advertisements**

**13.** The tenant must not display any sign or advertisement either on or within the property to be visible from outside the property unless:

    **13.1** the tenant has obtained consent from the landlord (not to be unreasonably withheld); or

    **13.2** the sign or advertisement is:

        **(a)** a usual trade sign or advertisement which is only displayed within the property; or

        **(b)** external fascia signage in the usual corporate style of the tenant's fascia signage from time to time and which is of a size and in a location previously approved by the landlord.

As it was originally drafted, this clause prevented the client from being able to advertise her business with the use of signage. This could potentially have a significant impact on Marcella's business. Amending this to the above will provide Marcella with the most security possible, while also taking into consideration the landlord's need to retain some level of control over the property. If Marcella seeks the landlord's consent and the landlord then refuses, they will need to provide reasoning for the refusal. If this occurs, it can then be considered further by the courts to determine whether this is reasonable. ❽

## COMMENTARY

❶ The first paragraph sets out the position of the client and identifies that to resolve the issue, something will need to change. It manages expectations and evidences to an examiner that the candidate can apply the law correctly to the client's situation.

❷ This section explicitly refers to the Landlord and Tenant Act 1954 and correctly applies the facts of the client's situation to identify its applicability. This is covered in *Revise SQE: Property Practice* and shows that the candidate can apply the Act and determine its implications in relation to the specific scenario.

③ This paragraph clearly identifies that Marcella has security of tenure and explains what this means for her. It also identifies disadvantages of going to court prior to suggesting alternatives, which is a good example of providing client-focused advice in a concise and precise manner. It is extremely important that clients are provided with all available options so that they can make informed decisions.

④ This paragraph concisely explains the option suggested, having taken into consideration the facts provided in the scenario. Section 26 notices can only be served if there is a fixed-term tenancy which is for more than a year. It needs to be served not less than 6 nor more than 12 months before the suggested commencement date. This response applies the law correctly to the client's situation and understands what the client wishes to achieve.

⑤ This paragraph clearly identifies that this option is not one that the client is likely to prefer by emphasising the client's preference to remain in the property. It provides the option to allow for the client to make an informed decision. However, it also shows the examiner that the candidate understands the client's wishes and can provide advice accordingly.

⑥ In this paragraph, it is clear that the client should be advised to choose the option of a s 26 notice. The candidate has taken into consideration all the facts and options available and has reached a reasonable conclusion based on the client's wishes. This option will also provide the most security and therefore the candidate applies the law correctly to the scenario. As such, this is likely to meet the assessment criteria for case and matter analysis.

⑦ This section considers what the client wants and provides a middle ground that might be acceptable to the landlord. Ultimately, landlords retain control to protect the value of the property. If there were any risk to the structure, the landlord may not consent. However, in this instance, the clause refers to internal, non-structural alterations. It is usual practice for these to be qualified or fully qualified covenants and is, therefore, a reasonable clause. It makes a further suggestion that can be made if the landlord does not approve, which shows an examiner the ability to provide client-focused advice.

⑧ Finally, this section again takes into consideration the client's wishes, but also follows the partner's instructions to consider the landlord and what they are likely to be agreeable to. It evidences to an examiner that the candidate can identify the landlord's concerns around impacting the value of the property and ensuring that control is retained, while balancing this with the client's needs.

## Does this answer meet the threshold?

The sample answer above includes all the components that the legal analysis and client-focused advice should cover. It correctly identifies that s 26 notices can only be served if there is a fixed-term tenancy, which is for more than a year, and appropriately explains legal terms in plain language. It provides the client with the best option based on her wish to remain in the property, in addition to the other relevant options to allow her to make an informed decision. It is likely to meet the threshold standard for the SQE2 case and matter analysis assessment.

Note how each of the assessment criteria for case and matter analysis are dealt with and, where appropriate, where the examiner is directed specifically to the areas of the advice which deal with those criteria. Remember that this is an assessment and that you need to show an examiner that you are meeting the criteria.

Now consider the second sample answer to question 2.

# ■ SAMPLE ANSWER 2 TO QUESTION 2

The Landlord and Tenant Act 1954 will apply here as Marcella has a business tenancy. **❶**

## 1.   What are the options available to Marcella?

It may be best to make a request under s 25 of the Landlord and Tenant Act 1954 Part II. However, this will mean that her rent goes up. But this would likely be within the next year anyway. **❷**

If Marcella is getting nowhere with the negotiations with the landlord, she could also issue a notice to quit providing that she gives one full month's notice. **❸**

Finally, there is also the option of doing nothing. If she waits until the expiry of the lease, and does nothing, then effectively at the end of the term, the lease will automatically end without the need for a notice. **❹**

Based on the above, I would advise Marcella to negotiate new terms for the lease under s 25 of the Landlord and Tenant Act. **❺**

## 2.   What alternative provisions would you suggest?

'The tenant may carry out internal, non-structural works only if it obtains consent, not to be unreasonably withheld.'

With the proposed amendments above, this will allow the landlord to keep a certain level of control. Unfortunately, it is going to be necessary to provide protection against the devaluation of the property. However, if the landlord agrees, the amended clause would still allow Marcella to put up the partitions. **❻**

'The tenant must not display any signs or advertisements on the property visible outside the property without the landlord's consent which is within the landlord's absolute discretion.'

It is important that the landlord does not risk the devaluation of property and therefore, it is likely that they will require complete control over any decisions in relation to signage on the property. This will provide them with the security they need but will also be beneficial to our client as, providing the landlord consents to it, she will be able to erect signs. **❼**

## COMMENTARY

**❶** While not entirely incorrect, this paragraph is very brief, and it does not provide any advice in relation to why it applies. It is important to show an examiner your ability to apply the law correctly to a client's situation, and without evidencing this you will probably not showcase this.

**❷** Not only is this incorrect, as s 25 relates to a landlord's notice to terminate the fixed-term tenancy, it is also poorly written. There is little explanation provided to an external examiner and the language used is not concise, precise or acceptable.

**❸** This is not applicable with fixed-term leases. A notice to quit only applies to periodic tenancies. This does not evidence to an examiner that the candidate can apply the law correctly to a client's situation. The paragraph also uses colloquial language in places and is unclear.

**❹** This paragraph is problematic as it provides incorrect advice that could potentially lead to a professional negligence claim. Under the Landlord and Tenant Act 1954, the common law rules do not apply in relation to effluxion of time. Under the Act, the lease would continue until it is terminated. In addition to this, the paragraph does not demonstrate an understanding of what the client wants to achieve, as she has specifically advised that she does not wish to give up the property. Remember to show the examiner that you understand your client's needs and have taken them into account in formulating the advice.

**⑤** Out of the options provided to the client, it would be in their best interests to negotiate with the landlord. However, this would be required under a s 26 notice on behalf of the tenant. This paragraph does not evidence to an examiner that the candidate can apply the law correctly to the client's situation.

**⑥** While this is not unreasonable, it is not the best starting point for negotiation as it would require Marcella to obtain permission from the landlord before making any internal alterations. The paragraph also advises that this is the only option available to Marcella, which is not good practice. It does not evidence to an examiner that the candidate is considering the client's wishes, and leans more towards the landlord's best interests. The absence of headings and reference to clause numbers for this part of the answer also makes the response appear less clear than Answer 1.

**⑦** This clause is a qualified covenant, which gives the landlord more control over the property. This is not what the client wants, and this response shows a lack of understanding of what the client wants to achieve. When negotiating, it is important to consider the landlord, but ultimately you need to act in your client's best interests.

## Does this answer meet the threshold?

It is unlikely that this second report would meet the threshold standard for the SQE2 case and matter analysis assessment criteria. It provides incorrect advice in relation to the common law rules and could result in a professional negligence claim being made against the firm. In addition, a qualified covenant would be more appropriate to suggest when acting on behalf of a landlord, as it provides them with more control. When acting on behalf of the client, this answer would restrict freedom and does not demonstrate acting in the best interests of the client.

## ■ KEY POINT CHECKLIST

This chapter has covered the following key knowledge points:
- The SQE2 assessment criteria for case and matter analysis and how to apply them in the context of property practice.
- A suggested structure for approaching an SQE2 case and matter analysis assessment question.
- How the different analysis and advice for planning enforcement issues and commercial leases given in sample answers would be likely or unlikely to meet the threshold standard for SQE2, with full commentary on the sample answers' strengths and weaknesses.

## ■ SUMMARY AND REFLECTION

It is important to take your time reviewing all the information given before making a start on your answer. Ensure that you create a plan including the legal points that you want to raise in your answer so that nothing is missed.

Remember that you are being assessed on your legal analysis in addition to providing client-focused advice. You will need to consider the appropriate law and analyse this to provide clear and applicable advice to the scenario.

Make sure you practise writing advice to the appropriate audience. In addition, remember to analyse all the options available before determining the most appropriate legal advice.

Now take the time to reflect and consider what you might still need to work on, and whether you feel completely confident in your legal analysis skills in the context of property practice.

# 2

# Legal research

## ■ MAKE SURE YOU KNOW

This chapter explores property law in the context of the skill of legal research, one of the skills that is assessed on the SQE2 assessments. Property law could arise in an SQE2 legal research assessment question on day two, to test both your knowledge of processes in property law and ability to apply land law principles. This revision guide should be read after familiarising yourself with the contents of *Revise SQE: Land Law* and *Revise SQE: Property Practice*. Delayed completion and breaches of leasehold covenants are developed further within this book to identify the ways in which SQE2 skills assessments incorporate the legal principles you will have learned for your SQE1 examinations.

Within this chapter you will find examples of how to investigate a problem for a client. You will discover how to identify potential remedies available to a client for both delayed completion and breaches of leasehold covenants, which could arise in the context of an SQE2 legal research assessment.

## ■ SQE ASSESSMENT ADVICE

As you work through this chapter, pay attention in your revision to:
- the legislation and case authorities provided for you to assist in the research task
- the structure used in the sample answers, for ease of use by the reader
- the way in which the advice is tailored to the recipient
- using precise, concise and acceptable language
- ensuring the law is applied correctly to the client's situation
- the way in which any ethical or professional conduct issues are identified and resolved.

See the Appendix for the SRA's performance indicators in legal research.

## ■ INTRODUCTION TO LEGAL RESEARCH IN PROPERTY PRACTICE

The SQE2 assessments aim to replicate scenarios from practice and will mirror daily aspects of the property law field. As with all areas of law, an essential aspect of practising in the field of property is the ability to clearly and accurately apply the law and provide legal advice. Your SQE2 legal research assessment will be to investigate a problem for a client. You will be given an email from a partner asking you to research an issue or issues, so that the partner can report back to the client. You will have to produce a written note explaining to the partner your legal reasoning and the key sources you rely on, as well as the advice the partner should give the client. While the question itself will give you some direction about the areas you need to cover in your advice, you will be required to apply your knowledge of those areas to the scenario and communicate the relevant advice to the partner, explaining your legal reasoning.

You will be provided with a number of sources to assist in answering the question and will be expected to determine which are appropriate to the scenario. Some of the sources provided will not be relevant – you will need to identify these and disregard them. You must base your answer on the relevant sources to successfully achieve the assessment criteria in legal research. This chapter will provide examples of how you can do this.

In order to succeed in your SQE2 legal research assessment, consider the question in a structured manner. Try adopting the following approach:

1. Once you have read the question, highlight the key legal authorities that will assist you in identifying the clients' options.
2. You can then form the structure of your answer, which will need to include the advice to be given to the client as well as the legal reasoning (citing key sources or authorities).
3. Write your answer, bearing in mind your audience and using appropriate terminology.
4. Review your answer, in line with the SQE2 legal research assessment criteria.

## Assessment technique

When identifying appropriate remedies for delayed completion, explore all options before determining which are the most appropriate for the facts of the matter. This is to ensure you do not miss any appropriate remedies that may be explored to appease the client as, ultimately, it could lead to a professional negligence claim being made against the firm.

## SQE2 legal research assessment criteria

Ensure that you follow these criteria when constructing your answer:

### Skills

1. Identify and use relevant sources and information.
2. Provide advice which is client-focused and addresses the client's problem.
3. Use clear, precise, concise and acceptable language.

### Application of law

4. Apply the law correctly to the client's situation.
5. Apply the law comprehensively to the client's situation, identifying any ethical and professional conduct issues and exercising judgement to resolve them honestly and with integrity.

In chapter 5 of *Revise SQE: Property Practice*, we considered the remedies for delayed completion, including key issues to look out for. Question 1 demonstrates how your knowledge of this topic could be tested in the context and format of an SQE2 legal research assessment. The sample questions below include six sources for you to consider, but bear in mind that the SQE2 assessment might include up to eight sources.

## ■ QUESTION 1

### Email to candidate

**From:** Partner
**Sent:** 3 June 202#
**To:** Candidate
**Subject:** Carolina Wieoski

My client, Carolina Wieoski, telephoned me today.

I am currently dealing with the purchase of a property for her, and the completion date was seven days ago. The contract is a standard Law Society 5th edition 2018 revision contract. The sellers were unable to complete the transaction and we therefore served a notice to complete for ten days' time. We are now due to complete in three days' time and the sellers have advised that they are ready, willing and able to complete.

It has now come to light that the sellers have not been entirely truthful. In the property information form, the seller specifically answered no to question 2.1 'Have there been any disputes or complaints regarding this property?' Carolina has advised that when she went to the property yesterday to measure up for curtains, she witnessed the seller arguing with a neighbour. A neighbour called Paul told her that it was over the right of way on the property, and that they had been 'at each other's throats for over a year'.

When I spoke to Carolina this morning, she was understandably upset by this and has advised that she does not want to continue with the purchase, as the seller lied on the property information form and she is now concerned about what she has been told and that there may be further issues that she is unaware of. She is also concerned about future disagreements with the neighbours if she continues with moving into the property.

**Carolina would like to know what options are available to her in relation to the misinformation that the seller has provided.**

**Could you please research the answer to this question, using the sources provided, and report back to me so that I can prepare my advice to Carolina. Please include your legal reasoning for my reference and ensure that you identify any key sources or authorities.**

Thanks

Partner

**Note to candidates:**

**Given the time constraints of this assessment, we have not provided the full text of some primary sources. Where the full text of a primary source is not provided, candidates may nevertheless cite the primary source on the basis it is referred to in one or more of the secondary sources provided and the full text can be checked at a later date.**

**Information displayed is as obtained on the date of search, for example purposes only. Information contained herein is not to be relied upon outside of the purposes of this sample question.**

**Attachments**

You have been provided with the following sources listed alphabetically in order of source name. The order of presentation is not intended as a guide to the order in which they should be consulted.

**PLEASE NOTE THAT PART OR ALL OF SOME OF THESE SOURCES MAY NOT BE RELEVANT.**

1.  *Hadley v Baxendale* (1854) 9 Exch 341
2.  Limitation Act 1980 ss 5, 15
3.  *McMeekin and another v Long and another* [2003] 2 EGLR 81
4.  Misrepresentation Act 1967 s 2
5.  *Raineri v Miles and another; (Wiejski and another, third parties)* [1980] 2 All ER 145
6.  Unfair Contract Terms Act 1977 s 8.

* * *

## Source 1

# *Hadley v Baxendale* (1854) 9 Exch 341

The first count of the declaration stated, that, before and at the time of the making by the defendants of the promises hereinafter mentioned, the plaintiffs carried on the business of millers and mealmen in copartnership, and were proprietors and occupiers of the City Steam-Mills, in the city of Gloucester, and were possessed of a steam-engine, by means of which they worked the said mills, and therein cleaned corn, and ground the same into meal, and dressed the same into flour, sharps, and bran, and a certain portion of the said steam-engine, to wit, the crank shaft of the said steam-engine, was broken and out of repair, whereby the said steam-engine was prevented from working, and the plaintiffs were desirous of having a new crank shaft made for the said mill, and had ordered the same of certain persons trading under the name of W. Joyce & Co., at Greenwich, in the country of Kent, who had contracted to make the said new shaft for the plaintiffs; but before they could complete the said new shaft it was necessary that the said broken shaft should be forwarded to their works at Greenwich, in order that the said new shaft might be made so as to fit the other parts of the said engine which were not injured, and so that it might be substituted for the said broken shaft; and the plaintiffs were desirous of sending the said broken shaft to the said W. Joyce & Co. for the purpose aforesaid; and the defendants, before and at the time of the making of the said promises, were common carriers of business of common carriers, under the name of 'Pickford & Co.'; and the plaintiffs, at the request of the defendants, delivered to them as such carriers the said broken shaft, to be conveyed by the defendants as such carriers from Gloucester to the said W. Joyce & Co., at Greenwich, and there to be delivered for the plaintiffs on the second day after the day of such delivery, for reward to the defendants; and in consideration thereof the defendants then promised the plaintiffs to convey the said broken shaft from Gloucester to Greenwich, and there on the said second day to deliver the same to the said W. Joyce & Co. for the plaintiffs. And although such second day elapsed before the commencement of this suit, yet the defendants did not nor would deliver the said broken shaft at Greenwich on the said second day, but wholly neglected and refused so to do for the space of seven days after the said shaft was so delivered to them as aforesaid.

The second count stated, that, the defendants being such carriers as aforesaid, the plaintiffs, at the request of the defendants, caused to be delivered to them as such carriers the said broken shaft, to be conveyed by the defendants from Gloucester aforesaid to the said W. Joyce & Co., at Greenwich, and there to be delivered by the defendants for the plaintiffs, within a reasonable time in that behalf, for reward to the defendants; and in consideration of the premises in this count mentioned, the defendants promised the plaintiffs to use due and proper care and diligence in and about the carrying and conveying the said broken shaft from Gloucester aforesaid to the said W. Joyce & Co., at Greenwich, and there delivering the same for the plaintiffs in a reasonable time then following for the carriage, conveyance, and delivery of the said broken shaft as aforesaid; and although such reasonable time elapsed long before the commencement of this suit, yet the defendants did not nor would use due or proper care or diligence in or about the carrying or conveying or delivering the said broken shaft as aforesaid, within such reasonable time as aforesaid, but wholly neglected and refused so to do; and by reason of the carelessness, negligence, and improper conduct of the defendants, the said broken shaft was not delivered for the plaintiffs to the said W. Joyce & Co., or at Greenwich, until the expiration of a long and unreasonable time after the defendants received the same as aforesaid, and after the time when the same should have been delivered for the plaintiffs; and by reason of the several premises, the completing of the said new shaft was delayed for five days, and the plaintiffs were prevented from working their said steam-mills, and from cleaning corn, and grinding the same into meal, and dressing the meal into flour, sharps, or bran, and from carrying on their said business as millers and mealmen for the space of five days beyond the time that they otherwise would have been prevented from so doing, and they thereby were unable to supply many of their customers with flour, sharps, and bran during that period, and were obliged to buy flour to supply some of their other customers, and lost the mans and opportunity of selling flour, sharps, and bran, and were deprived of gains and profits which otherwise would have accrued to them, and were unable to employ their workmen, to whom they were compelled to pay wages during that period, and were otherwise injured, and the plaintiffs claim [£300].

The defendants pleaded *non assumpserunt* [denied liability] to the first count; and to the second payment of [£25] into Court in satisfaction of the plaintiffs' claim under that count. The plaintiffs entered a *nolle prosequi* [unwilling to pursue] as to the first count; and as to the second plea, they replied that the sum paid into the Court was not enough to satisfy the plaintiffs' claim in respect thereof; upon which replication issue was joined.

At the trial before Crompton, J., at the last Gloucester Assizes, it appeared that the plaintiffs carried on an extensive business as millers at Gloucester; and that, on the 11th of May, their mill was stopped by a breakage of the crank shaft by which the mill was worked. The steam-engine was manufactured by Messrs. Joyce & Co., the engineers, at Greenwich, and it became necessary to send the shaft as a pattern for a new one to Greenwich. The fracture was discovered on the 12th, and on the 13th the plaintiffs sent one of their servants to the office of the defendants, who are the well-known carriers trading under the name of Pickford & Co., for the purpose of having the shaft carried to Greenwich. The plaintiffs' servant told the clerk that the mill was stopped, and that the shaft must be sent immediately; and in answer to the inquiry when the shaft would be taken, the answer was, that if it was sent up by twelve o'clock an day, it would be delivered at Greenwich on the following day. On the following day the shaft was taken by the defendants, before noon, for the purpose of being conveyed to Greenwich, and the sum of [£2 4 shillings] was paid for its carriage for the whole distance; at the same time the defendants' clerk was told that a special entry, if required, should be made to hasten its delivery. The delivery of the shaft at Greenwich was delayed by some neglect; and the consequence was, that the plaintiffs did not receive the new shaft for several days after they would otherwise have done, and the working of their mill was thereby delayed, and they thereby lost the profits they would otherwise have received.

On the part of the defendants, it was objected that these damages were too remote, and that the defendants were not liable with respect to them. The learned Judge left the case generally to the jury, who found a verdict with [£25] damages beyond the amount paid into Court.

Whateley . . . obtained a rule nisi for a new trial, on the ground of misdirection.

The judgment of the Court was now delivered by

ALDERSON, B.

We think that there ought to be a new trial in this case; but, in so doing, we deem it to be expedient and necessary to state explicitly the rule which the Judge, at the next trial, ought, in our opinion, to direct the jury to be governed by when they estimate the damages.

It is, indeed, of the last importance that we should do this; for, if the jury are left without any definite rule to guide them, it will, in such cases as these, manifestly lead to the greatest injustice. The Courts have done this on several occasions; and, in *Blake v Midland Rail Co* (18 QB 93) the Court granted a new trial on this very ground, that the rule had not been definitely laid down to the jury by the learned Judge at nisi prius. In *Alder v Keighley* (2) POLLOCK, CB, said (15 M & W at p120):

'There are certain established rules', this Court says, in Alder v. Keighley (15 M & W 117), 'according to which the jury ought to find...and here there is a clear rule, that the amount which would have been received if the contract had been kept, is the measure of damages if the contract is broken.'

Now we think the proper rule in such a case as the present is this: where two parties have made a contract which one of them has broken, the damages which the other party ought to receive in respect of such breach of contract should be such as may fairly and reasonably be considered either arising naturally, i.e., according to the usual course of things, from such breach of contract itself, or such as may reasonably be supposed to have been in the contemplation of both parties, at the time they made the contract, as the probable result of the breach of it. Now, if the special circumstances under which the contract was actually made were communicated by the plaintiffs to the defendants, and thus known to both parties, the damages resulting from the breach of such a contract, which they would reasonably contemplate, would be the amount of injury which would ordinarily follow from a breach of contract under these special circumstances so known and communicated. But, on the other hand, if these special circumstances were wholly unknown to the party breaking the contract, he, at the most, could only be supposed to have had in his contemplation the amount of injury which would arise generally, and in the real multitude of cases not affected by any special circumstances, from such a breach of contract. For such loss would neither have flowed naturally from the breach of this contract in the great multitude of such cases occurring under ordinary circumstances, nor were the special circumstances, which, perhaps, would have made it a reasonable and natural consequence of such breach of contract, communicated to or known by the defendants. The Judge ought, therefore, to have told the jury that, upon the facts then before them, they ought not to take the loss of profits into consideration at all in estimating the damages. There must, therefore, be a new trial in this case.

Rule absolute.

*    *    *

## Source 2

Contains public sector information licensed under the Open Government Licence v3.0.

# Limitation Act 1980

# 1980 Chapter 58

PART I ORDINARY TIME LIMITS FOR DIFFERENT CLASSES OF ACTION

*Time limits under Part I subject to extension or exclusion under Part II*

*Actions founded on simple contract*

**5    Time limit for actions founded on simple contract.**

An action founded on simple contract shall not be brought after the expiration of six years from the date on which the cause of action accrued.

**Modifications etc. (not altering text)**

**C13** S. 5 extended (11.11.1999 with effect as mentioned in s. 10(2)(3) of the amending Act) by 1999 c. 31, **ss. 7(3)**, 10(2)(3)

*Actions to recover land and rent*

**15    Time limit for actions to recover land.**

(1) No action shall be brought by any person to recover any land after the expiration of twelve years from the date on which the right of action accrued to him or, if it first accrued to some person through whom he claims, to that person.
(2) Subject to the following provisions of this section, where—
    (a) the estate or interest claimed was an estate or interest in reversion or remainder or any other future estate or interest and the right of action to recover the land accrued on the date on which the estate or interest fell into possession by the determination of the preceding estate or interest; and
    (b) the person entitled to the preceding estate or interest (not being a term of years absolute) was not in possession of the land on that date.
    No action shall be brought by the person entitled to the succeeding estate or interest after the expiration of 12 years from the date on which the right of action accrued to the person entitled to the preceding estate or interest or six years from the date on which the right of action accrued to the person entitled to the succeeding estate or interest, whichever period last expires.
(3) Subsection (2) above shall not apply to any estate or interest which falls into possession on the determination of an entailed interest, and which might have been barred by the person entitled to the entailed interest.
(4) No person shall bring an action to recover any estate or interest in land under an assurance taking effect after the right of action to recover the land had accrued to the person by whom the assurance was made or some person through whom he claimed or some person entitled to a preceding estate or interest, unless the action is brought within the period during which the person by whom the assurance was made could have brought such an action.

(5) Where any person is entitled to any estate or interest in land in possession and, while so entitled, is also entitled to any future estate or interest in that land, and his right to recover the estate or interest in possession is barred under this Act, no action shall be brought by that person, or by any person claiming through him, in respect of the future estate or interest, unless in the meantime possession of the land has been recovered by a person entitled to an intermediate estate or interest.

(6) Part I of Schedule 1 to this Act contains provisions for determining the date of accrual of rights of action to recover land in the cases there mentioned.

(7) Part II of that Schedule contains provisions modifying the provisions of this section in their application to actions brought by, or by a person claiming through, the Crown or any spiritual or eleemosynary corporation sole.

**Modifications etc. (not altering text)**

**C15** S. 15 restricted (31.10.1994) by 1994 c. 21, **ss. 10(2)(a)(4)**, 68(2)(a); S.I. 1994/2553, **art. 2**

S. 15 excluded (13.10.2003) by The Proceeds of Crime Act 2002 (c. 9), ss. 96(1), 136(2) (with s. 129); S.I. 2003/1725, **art. 2**

\* \* \*

**Source 3**

## *McMeekin and another v Long and another* [2003] 2 EGLR 81

Sale of land — Misrepresentation — Fraudulent misrepresentation — Seller's property information form — Representation that 'neighbours were good and friendly' — Representation stating no disputes — Disputes between sellers and neighbours preceding sale — Disputes maintained against buyers — Whether misrepresentation by sellers about disputes — Whether misrepresentation fraudulent — Whether buyers relying upon misrepresentations

In 1999, the claimants purchased a house from the defendants. They subsequently alleged fraudulent, negligent and/or innocent misrepresentation upon which they relied in purchasing the property. They relied upon two matters that arose prior to the contract. First, when the claimants were viewing the property, the defendants made a verbal representation that the 'neighbours were good and friendly'. Second, in the seller's property information form (SPIF), the defendants replied 'no' to two questions asking about disputes with neighbours and about complaints. The claimants contended that the defendants had not revealed that, during their ownership of the property, they had been involved in disputes with Mr and Mrs C both about parking on an access road and about rubbish: Mr and Mrs C were the owners of the access and of a dwelling nearby. The defendants argued that there had been a dispute. However, following legal advice that Mr and Mrs C had been correct about the car-parking issue, which advice the defendants accepted, no further dispute arose. The defendants also maintained that, although there had been an incident concerning rubbish, it did not constitute a dispute.

Held: The claim was allowed. The defendants had made a fraudulent misrepresentation. Disputes with neighbours had occurred prior to the misrepresentation and the defendants should have recognised that they constituted disputes that they were required to disclose in the SPIF. After the claimants had purchased the property, the disputes continued; there was an atmosphere of constant confrontation between Mr and Mrs C and the other occupants of houses in the road. The problem suffered by the defendants when they had lived in the property was precisely the kind of information that they were obliged to disclose to a potential purchaser. The defendants knew, or ought to have known, that these matters constituted disputes. The questions on the SPIF were expressed in clear and simple language that was designed for everyone to understand. The claimants had relied upon the misrepresentations in purchasing the property.

*   *   *

## Source 4

# Misrepresentation Act 1967

## 2    Damages for misrepresentation.

(1) Where a person has entered into a contract after a misrepresentation has been made to him by another party thereto and as a result thereof he has suffered loss, then, if the person making the misrepresentation would be liable to damages in respect thereof had the misrepresentation been made fraudulently, that person shall be so liable notwithstanding that the misrepresentation was not made fraudulently, unless he proves that he had reasonable ground to believe and did believe up to the time the contract was made the facts represented were true.

(2) Where a person has entered into a contract after a misrepresentation has been made to him otherwise than fraudulently, and he would be entitled, by reason of the misrepresentation, to rescind the contract, then, if it is claimed, in any proceedings arising out of the contract, that the contract ought to be or has been rescinded, the court or arbitrator may declare the contract subsisting and award damages in lieu of rescission, if of opinion that it would be equitable to do so, having regard to the nature of the misrepresentation and the loss that would be caused by it if the contract were upheld, as well as to the loss that rescission would cause to the other party.

(3) Damages may be awarded against a person under subsection (2) of this section whether or not he is liable to damages under subsection (1) thereof, but where he is so liable any award under the said subsection (2) shall be taken into account in assessing his liability under the said subsection (1).

[F1 (4) This section does not entitle a person to be paid damages in respect of a misrepresentation if the person has a right to redress under Part 4A of the Consumer Protection from Unfair Trading Regulations 2008 (SI 2008/1277) in respect of the conduct constituting the misrepresentation.

(5) Subsection (4) does not prevent a debtor from bringing a claim under section 75(1) of the Consumer Credit Act 1974 against a creditor under a debtor-creditor-supplier agreement in a case where, but for subsection (4), the debtor would have a claim against the supplier in respect of a misrepresentation (and, where section 75 of that Act would otherwise apply, it accordingly applies as if the debtor had a claim against the supplier).]

## Textual amendments

[F1 S. 2 (4)(5) inserted (1.10.2014) by The Consumer Protection (Amendment) Regulations 2014 (S.I. 2014/870), regs. 1(3),]

[F2 3 Avoidance of provision excluding liability for misrepresentation.

[F3 (1)] If a contract contains a term which would exclude or restrict—
(a) any liability to which a party to a contract may be subject by reason of any misrepresentation made by him before the contract was made; or
(b) any remedy available to another party to the contract by reason of such a misrepresentation,

that term shall be of no effect except in so far as it satisfies the requirement of reasonableness as stated in section 11 (1) of the M1 Unfair Contract Terms Act 1977; and it is for those claiming that the term satisfies that requirement to show that it does.]

[F4 (2) This section does not apply to a term in a consumer contract within the meaning of Part 2 of the Consumer Rights Act 2015 (but see the provision made about such contracts in section 62 of that Act).]

## Textual amendments

F2 S. 3 substituted by Unfair Contract Terms Act 1977 (c. 50), s. 8(1)

F3 Word in s. 3 inserted (1.10.2015) by Consumer Rights Act 2015 (c. 15), s. 100(5), Sch. 4 para. 1(2); S.I. 2015/1630, art. 3(g) (with art. 6(1))

F4 S. 3(2) inserted (1.10.2015) by Consumer Rights Act 2015 (c. 15), s. 100(5), Sch. 4 para. 1(3); S.I. 2015/1630, art. 3(g) (with art. 6(1))

* * *

**Source 5**

## *Raineri v Miles and another; (Wiejski and another, third parties)* [1980] 2 All ER 145

By a contract incorporating the Law Society's Conditions of Sale (1973 Revision) the third parties agreed to sell a house to the defendants. The contract provided that the purchase should be completed on or before 12 July 1977, when vacant possession was to be given to the defendants. At the same time the defendants agreed to sell the house in which they were then living to the plaintiff, that contract also providing for completion with vacant possession on 12 July. In neither case was the time for completion expressed to be of the essence of the contract. On 11 July the defendants were told that the third parties could not complete their contract with them on the following day. The defendants immediately informed the plaintiff's solicitors, but the plaintiff himself had already vacated his previous house and was on the road with his furniture intending to take possession of his new house. In consequence of the third parties' failure to complete their contract with the defendants on 12 July, the defendants were prevented from giving the plaintiff vacant possession and could not complete their contract with him on that day in accordance with its terms. On 13 July the defendants, being then ready, able and willing to complete their contract with the third parties, gave them notice, pursuant to condition 19[a] of the conditions of sale, to complete the contract by 11 August. The contract between the defendants and the third parties was duly completed on that day. The defendants' contract with the plaintiff was also completed on that day and the plaintiff was let into possession. Between 12 July and 11 August the plaintiff incurred expense in providing himself and his family with living accommodation for which he recovered damages from the defendants. The defendants served the third parties with a third party notice claiming indemnity against the plaintiff's claim on the ground of the third parties' failure to give vacant possession on or before 12 July. The judge dismissed the third party proceedings. On an appeal by the defendants the third parties contended that, where time was not of the essence, the contract only required completion on the date fixed for completion or within a reasonable time thereafter and that, since they had completed in a reasonable time, they had not committed a breach of the contract and so were not liable in damages for the delay. They further contended that the effect of the notice to complete was to substitute for 12 July a new date for completion and that they had fulfilled the contracts as so varied. The Court of Appeal ([1979] 3 All ER 763) rejected these contentions and allowed the defendants' appeal. The third parties appealed to the House of Lords.

[a] Condition 19, so far as material, is set out at p 148 f to j, post

Held (Viscount Dilhorne dissenting)—The appeal would be dismissed for the following reasons—

(1) Failure to complete a contract for the sale of land on the date specified in the contract constituted a breach thereof and entitled the other party to recover any damages properly attributable thereto, provided that the failure to complete was not due to some conveyancing difficulty or some difficulty with regard to title, notwithstanding that the time for completion was not expressed to be of the essence of the contract, for the fact that time had not been declared to be of the essence did not mean that the express date for completion could be supplanted by the court's treating it as a mere target date and in effect enabling the defaulting party to insert into the contractual provision some such words as 'or within a reasonable time'. The effect of s 41[b] of the Law of Property Act 1925 was not to negative the existence of a breach of contract where one had occurred but in certain circumstances to bar any assertion that the breach amounted to a repudiation of the contract. It followed therefore that, by failing to complete with vacant possession on 12 July, the third parties had committed both at law and in equity a breach of their contract with the defendants, but although that breach could not have been relied on by the defendants as a ground for avoiding an action for specific performance it afforded no ground for construing the contract otherwise than in accordance with its clear terms (see p 153 j, p 154 b c, p 155 f, p 157 f, p 159 c, p 160 c d, p 161 f g, p 163 d e, p 164 d e and p 165 c to f, post); *Phillips v Lamdin* [1949] 1 All ER 770 applied.

(2) The service of a notice to complete under condition 19, which could only be served after the date fixed for completion had passed, by which time the innocent party had an accrued right to damages, added to the remedies available to the party serving the notice against the defaulting party in the event of the party served failing to comply with it without excluding the existing remedies. Accordingly the defendants had not been deprived of any cause of action in damages against the third parties which had accrued before they served the notice to complete (see p 157 h to p 158 b, p 159 c, p 164 h j and p 165 a to f, post).

(3) The fact that the failure of the third parties to complete was due to their inability to raise the necessary finance afforded no defence to the defendants' entitlement to

be compensated (see p 158 j to p 159 a and c, p 164 g h and p 165 c to f, post); *The Edison* [1933] All ER Rep 144 and *Thomas v Kensington* [1942] 2 All ER 263 applied.

Decision of the Court of Appeal [1979] 3 All ER 763 affirmed.

[b] Section 41 is set out at p 149 d, post

\* \* \*

## Source 6

Contains public sector information licensed under the Open Government Licence v3.0.

## Unfair Contract Terms Act 1977

8    X1 Misrepresentation.

(1) In the Misrepresentation Act 1967, the following is substituted for section 3—
'3 Avoidance of provision excluding liability for misrepresentation.
If a contract contains a term which would exclude or restrict—
(a) any liability to which a party to a contract may be subject by reason of any misrepresentation made by him before the contract was made; or
(b) any remedy available to another party to the contract by reason of such a misrepresentation, that term shall be of no effect except in so far as it satisfies the requirement of reasonableness as stated in section 11(1) of the Unfair Contract Terms Act 1977; and it is for those claiming that the term satisfies that requirement to show that it does.'
(2) The same section is substituted for section 3 of the Misrepresentation Act (Northern Ireland) 1967.

\* \* \*

## ■ YOUR TURN

Have a go at answering question 1, remembering the guidance on pages 19-20.
• Refer to the structured approach in the SRA's assessment criteria on page 20.
• Create a list of the most relevant legal authorities to assist with your answer and determine the correct legal advice to provide.
• Timings are important: you will need to prepare and write your answer in one hour.

| SQE1 Functioning legal knowledge link |
| --- |
| Remember from chapter 5 of *Revise SQE: Property Practice* that any contractual compensation awarded to a client will need to be deducted from the total amount of common law contractual damages to ensure that there is no 'double recovery'. |

## EVALUATING YOUR ANSWER

When you have attempted question 1, mark it yourself against the SQE2 legal research assessment criteria. Do you think your attempt met the threshold standard?

Now compare your attempt with the following key legal points and two sample answers to question 1. A circled number indicates that commentary is provided for this part of the answer. The commentary will explain whether the sample is likely to meet the threshold SQE2 standard.

In the assessment, part or all of the sources could be relevant to the question. It is imperative that you are able to identify which sources are not relevant.

---

➡️**Key legal points: Question 1**

In this assessment, part, or all, of the following sources are relevant to the question:

- *Hadley v Baxendale* (1854) 9 Exch 341
- *McMeekin and another v Long and another* [2003] 2 EGLR 81
- Misrepresentation Act 1967 s 2
- *Raineri v Miles and another; (Wiejski and another, third parties)* [1980] 2 All ER 145.

The following sources are not relevant to the question:

- Limitation Act 1980 ss 5, 15
- Unfair Contract Terms Act 1977 s 8.

**Key legal points** include the following:

- It is likely that Carolina will be able to bring a claim for misrepresentation and therefore may be able to rescind the contract under s 2 of the Misrepresentation Act 1967 and claim damages.
- *Hadley v Baxendale* (1854) and *Raineri v Miles* [1980] are both relevant to identify that there has been a breach of the contract. If unsuccessful in her misrepresentation claim, Carolina will still be able to recover losses stemming from the breach.
- *McMeekin and another v Long and another* [2003] is also relevant as it takes the law one step further to identify false information in properly information forms as misrepresentation.
- Serving a notice to complete will make time of the essence of the contract so that if the new completion date is not met, it will allow for the termination of the contract immediately. In addition to this, it will allow the innocent party to recover the deposit (if applicable) and claim for damages alongside interest to cover their losses.
- Compensation for the delay of completion is awarded regardless as to whether the party has suffered any loss. If there are losses suffered that exceed the compensation, these can be recovered in a claim for breach of contract. Damages for breach of contract are assessed based on the contractual principles established in *Hadley v Baxendale*. Any losses stemming from the breach of contract are able to be claimed for. However, it is important to note, under SC7.2 (SC: Standard conditions of sale under the Law Society Contract 5th Edition, 2018 revision) credit must be awarded for any compensation previously received.
- Under SC7.1, there is a right to rescind the contract for misrepresentation. (Where this is exercised, the buyer can recover the deposit alongside accrued interest, but will need to return documentation to the seller alongside putting the parties back in the position they were in prior to the exchange of contracts.) This can include compensation to balance the parties' positions. However, this effectively means that additional damages will not be payable as there will then have been no breach.
- There are various types of misrepresentation: fraudulent (deliberate), negligent (careless but not deliberate) and innocent (by mistake). When bringing a claim for fraudulent or negligent misrepresentation, remedies sought can be rescission and damages. However, when established that it is innocent misrepresentation, the only remedy available will be recission.

# ■ SAMPLE ANSWER 1 TO QUESTION 1

I understand that Carolina wants to know what options are available to her in relation to the breach of contract and misrepresentation that she has experienced in the purchase of a property.

I have researched remedies available in relation to delayed completion and it is apparent that a breach of contract occurred when the completion date was delayed by the sellers. In the case of *Raineri v Miles*, it was held that a failure to complete a contract for the sale of land on the date specified in the contract constituted a breach thereof and entitled the other party to recover any damages properly attributable. As such, it is clear that Carolina would be entitled to damages. ❶

In addition to this, she may be able to recover any losses that have stemmed from the breach of contract under the principles established in *Hadley v Baxendale*. In this case, the plaintiffs were deprived of gains and profits due to delayed completion through no fault of their own. As a result of this, they suffered losses stemming from the breach of contractual completion, such as being unable to employ their workmen, to whom they were compelled to pay wages during that period and otherwise suffered loss. It was held that they were able to recover these additional losses as they stemmed from the breach of contract. ❷

I understand that the notice to complete has been sent and the sellers have confirmed that they are ready, willing and able to complete. As such, it makes time of the essence. I have researched whether Carolina will be able to rescind the contract, and she would only be able to do this if the sellers did not comply with the notice to complete. As they have indicated that they are now in a position to complete, she will not be able to rescind the contract for the breach of contract (ie the delay to completion). However, she may be able to rescind the contract if there was a case of misrepresentation, fraud or mistake. ❸

Section 2(1) of the Misrepresentation Act states that where there has been misrepresentation, a party would be entitled to claim rescission of contract and/or damages as a result of that. However, recission is an equitable remedy and it is important to manage the client's expectations in relation to this. If it is held to be an innocent misrepresentation, under s 2(2) Carolina can only rescind the contract. The court can award damages in lieu of rescission of contract for negligent or innocent misrepresentation, but it is important to note that it is at their discretion. This would mean that Carolina could only claim for recission (if claiming innocent misrepresentation). ❹

We should therefore advise Carolina that it is likely that she will be able to bring a claim against the seller for misrepresentation due to the misinformation provided in the property information form, and rescind the contract and recover damages stemming from this loss providing it is fraudulent or negligent misrepresentation. It is important to advise Carolina not to go ahead with completion as if she does, it will be deemed as acceptance and therefore will be a bar to rescission. ❺

In addition, Carolina is further supported with the ruling in *McMeekin and another v Long and another*. In this case it was held that the defendants had made a fraudulent misrepresentation and that the questions on the property information form were expressed in clear and simple language that was designed for everyone to understand. The claimants had relied upon the misrepresentations in purchasing the property. This further strengthens Carolina's claim as the other neighbour, Paul, advised that this situation has been ongoing over the last year. It is therefore evident that a misrepresentation has occurred. *McMeekin* would therefore support Carolina's claim for fraudulent or negligent misrepresentation as it highlights that the seller should not be able to claim innocent misrepresentation based on the above facts. **6**

## COMMENTARY

**1** The beginning of this paragraph clearly states the current circumstances, that the client will be entitled to recover damages. *Raineri v Mills* identified that if there was a failure to complete the transaction on the contractual date, it should be treated as a breach and would entitle the injured party to recover damages suffered.

**2** This section uses a logical structure following the previous point in identifying the rule in *Hadley v Baxendale*. Remember, at this point, not only can the client recover damages but she can also recover losses stemming from the breach of contract. The candidate uses client-friendly, clear language to convey facts and information effectively.

**3** It is clear from the initial information that the correct procedure has been followed and the sellers are ready, willing and able to complete on the revised date. As such, although the client will be able to recover damages and losses stemming from the breach, the only way that she would be able to rescind the contract would be to bring a claim for misrepresentation. The candidate has demonstrated an understanding of the client's problem from the client's perspective, for example, acknowledging that the client is concerned about the neighbours' dispute and wants to rescind the contract. This paragraph demonstrates to the examiner that the candidate can apply the law correctly to the individual scenario.

**4** and **5** These paragraphs set out that it is possible for the client to bring a claim for misrepresentation under the Misrepresentation Act. It will probably be easier to prove negligent misrepresentation, as it is unlikely that the seller would be able to demonstrate that they believed the statement to be true. When bringing a claim for fraudulent misrepresentation, it may be problematic to establish sufficient evidence to prove it. It is important to manage the client's expectations in relation to this and communicate effectively. In this case, there is evidence to suggest that deliberate misinformation was provided in the property information form which would appear to satisfy the requirements under the Misrepresentation Act. The candidate rightly notes that if Carolina was to go ahead with completion (now the sellers are ready, willing and able), it would effectively mean that she is accepting the breach and therefore there would be a bar to rescission. In that instance, it is likely that she will then be awarded damages in place of rescission, which is not what the client wants. This is a client-focused response.

**6** The candidate has identified the relevant fundamental legal principles and case (*McMeekin*), and applied them correctly to the facts of the client's case: the candidate advises that Carolina should be able to claim for fraudulent or negligent misrepresentation with rescission of contract alongside damages. It is important to note here the interpretation of the Act in accordance with the legislation. The facts and evidence from the neighbours would probably support a claim for fraudulent or negligent misrepresentation. The guidance clearly identifies that it would be unlikely that the seller could claim innocent misrepresentation and as such, Carolina should be able to claim for rescission of contract and damages. The candidate's legal analysis is sufficiently detailed in the context of the client's case: the candidate has explained the different types of misrepresentation and why it is likely that Carolina will be able to claim for fraudulent or negligent misrepresentation. Remember that if the client was bringing a claim for innocent misrepresentation, while she would be able to rescind the contract she would not be entitled to damages as the remedies available under s 2(2) – rescission OR damages and damages – are at the court's discretion. This response shows the examiner that the candidate can interpret the relevant law and provide advice accordingly.

## Does this answer meet the threshold?

The sample answer above includes all the remedies that may be available to the client given their circumstances. It appropriately identifies that recission of the contract is a discretionary remedy by the court and effectively manages the client's expectations. It has selected the relevant sources and applied them to the facts to provide reasonable advice to the client. It is therefore likely to meet the threshold standard for the SQE2 legal research assessment.

Now consider the second sample answer to question 1.

## ■ SAMPLE ANSWER 2 TO QUESTION 1

The sellers breached the contract when they delayed completion and therefore Carolina will be able to recover any and all losses that she has suffered under the principles in *Hadley v Baxendale*. ❶

I know that you sent the notice to complete, and the sellers have confirmed they are ready to complete, so the only options are either to claim under the Unfair Contract Terms Act which states:

(1) In the Misrepresentation Act 1967, the following is substituted for section 3—
    '3 Avoidance of provision excluding liability for misrepresentation.
    If a contract contains a term which would exclude or restrict—
    (a) any liability to which a party to a contract may be subject by reason of any misrepresentation made by him before the contract was made; or
    (b) any remedy available to another party to the contract by reason of such a misrepresentation, that term shall be of no effect except in so far as it satisfies the requirement of reasonableness as stated in section 11(1) of the Unfair Contract Terms Act 1977; and it is for those claiming that the term satisfies that requirement to show that it does.'
(2) The same section is substituted for section 3 of the Misrepresentation Act (Northern Ireland) 1967. ❷

Or bring a claim for misrepresentation.

We should advise the client that she may be able to claim that the contract was an unfair contract or bring a claim against the seller for misrepresentation due to the misinformation provided in the property information form and rescind the contract but not recover damages stemming from this loss. ❸

Section 2 of the Misrepresentation Act states that where there has been misrepresentation (other than fraudulently), a party can cancel the contract as a result of that misrepresentation:

(1) Where a person has entered into a contract after a misrepresentation has been made to him by another party thereto and as a result thereof he has suffered loss, then, if the person making the misrepresentation would be liable to damages in respect thereof had the misrepresentation been made fraudulently, that person shall be so liable notwithstanding that the misrepresentation was not made fraudulently, unless he proves that he had reasonable ground to believe and did believe up to the time the contract was made the facts represented were true.
(2) Where a person has entered into a contract after a misrepresentation has been made to him otherwise than fraudulently, and he would be entitled, by reason of the misrepresentation, to rescind the contract, then, if it is claimed, in any proceedings

arising out of the contract, that the contract ought to be or has been rescinded, the court or arbitrator may declare the contract subsisting and award damages in lieu of rescission, if of opinion that it would be equitable to do so, having regard to the nature of the misrepresentation and the loss that would be caused by it if the contract were upheld, as well as to the loss that rescission would cause to the other party. ④

Under s 15 of the Limitation Act 1980, no action shall be brought by any person to recover any land after the expiration of 12 years from the date on which the right of action accrued to him or, if it first accrued to some person through whom he claims, to that person. Carolina would therefore have 12 years to bring a claim against the seller for misrepresentation, so she does not need to panic as there is plenty of time. She should get some statements from the other neighbours to prove that a misrepresentation has occurred. If we go down the route of claiming misrepresentation, it is likely that Carolina will be able to rescind the contract but will not be able to recover any damages. ⑤

## COMMENTARY

① This is incorrect. The rule in *Hadley v Baxendale* identifies that losses stemming from the breach are recoverable. However, these need to be reasonable, and the client would need to evidence that they are mitigating their losses. This paragraph is misguided and would not provide sound advice to the client.

② and ③ The Unfair Contract Terms Act does not apply to this scenario. The contract is a standard Law Society 5th edition 2018 revision contract and would therefore not fall under the terms of this Act. There is no clear guidance to justify why it is an option. Although the answer notes that the Misrepresentation Act is relevant, it is unlikely that this would meet the SQE2 legal research assessment criteria as the candidate does not identify or use relevant sources and information.

④ This enquiry is an incomplete interpretation of the Misrepresentation Act. It is important to remember that recission of contracts is an equitable remedy and, as such, aims to put an innocent party into the position they were in prior to the breach/ misrepresentation. This response would have the potential to provide the client with incomplete advice and therefore could lead to a professional misconduct claim against the firm. It would not satisfy the SQE2 legal research assessment criteria as it does not apply the law correctly to the client's situation.

⑤ Although the Limitation Act provides for the length of time the client would have to bring a claim, this client has not requested advice on this matter, so this response does not therefore address the client's questions. This paragraph also provides incorrect advice, as the contract was not made by deed and therefore the limitation period would be 6 years and not 12. If this information was provided to the client, they could potentially bring a claim against the firm for professional negligence if they relied on the advice and missed limitation. However, given the client's circumstances and that she wants to withdraw from the purchase altogether, this is not relevant to the partner's request for specific advice, and is therefore unlikely to evidence to an examiner that this answer satisfies the SQE2 legal research assessment criteria.

### Does this answer meet the threshold?

It is unlikely that this would meet the threshold standard for the SQE2 legal research assessment. When assessed against the SQE2 legal research assessment criteria, it does not apply the relevant law precisely, it is not clear and it has omissions that have affected the advice provided. Incorrectly interpreting the Limitation Act has the potential to lead the client to be statute-barred from bringing a claim, which could effectively be seen as professional negligence. The answer does not identify all relevant sources and includes some that are not applicable to the client's scenario.

In chapter 8 of **Revise SQE: Property Practice**, we considered the remedies for breach of leasehold covenants, including key issues to look out for. Question 2 below demonstrates how your knowledge of this topic could be tested in the context and format of an SQE2 legal research assessment.

# ■ QUESTION 2

## Email to candidate

**From:** Partner
**Sent:** 6 July 202#
**To:** Candidate
**Subject:** Guillermo Cuesta

My client, Guillermo Cuesta, telephoned me today.

He owns the freehold to a leasehold complex and is currently having problems with one of his tenants. All leases within the complex were created in 2005 and the lease in question is a 99-year lease. The original landlord sold the freehold to Guillermo in 2010. The original lessee sold the leasehold title to the current tenants in 2015. Guillermo has advised me that there has been a breach of the repairing covenants in the lease and wants to know what his options are in relation to this.

He said that due to this breach, the overall freehold has been devalued. He has received quotes from a construction specialist, who has estimated the cost of repairs at £30,000.

Guillermo has also advised that he has no plans to structurally alter or demolish the property; he just wants the property value to be reinstated to its previous value.

**Guillermo would like to know what options are available to him in relation to the breach of repairing covenants.**

**Could you please research the answer to this question, using the sources provided, and report back to me so that I can prepare my advice to Guillermo. Please include your legal reasoning for my reference and ensure that you identify any key sources or authorities.**

Thanks

Partner

**Note to candidates:**

**Given the time constraints of this assessment, we have not provided the full text of some primary sources. Where the full text of a primary source is not provided, candidates may nevertheless cite the primary source on the basis it is referred to in one or more of the secondary sources provided and the full text can be checked at a later date.**

**Information displayed is as obtained on the date of search, for example purposes only. Information contained herein is not to be relied upon outside of the purposes of this sample question.**

**Attachments**

You have been provided with the following sources listed alphabetically in order of source name. The order of presentation is not intended as a guide to the order in which they should be consulted.

**PLEASE NOTE THAT PART OR ALL OF SOME OF THESE SOURCES MAY NOT BE RELEVANT.**

1.  *Avonridge Property Co Ltd v Mashru* [2005] UKHL 70
2.  *Jervis v Harris* [1996] Ch 195
3.  Landlord and Tenant Act 1927 s 18
4.  Landlord and Tenant (Covenants) Act 1995 s 3
5.  Law of Property Act 1925 s 146
6.  Leasehold Property (Repairs) Act 1938 s 1.

\*  \*  \*

**Source 1**

Contains public sector information licensed under the Open Government Licence v3.0.

## *Avonridge Property Co Ltd v Mashru* [2005] UKHL 70190

Lord Nicholls of Birkenhead

1.  This appeal raises a question on the effect of the Landlord and Tenant (Covenants) Act 1995. A sublease invariably contains a covenant by the lessor to pay the rent due under the head lease. Before the enactment of the 1995 Act a lessor could, by the use of appropriate wording, limit his liability under such a covenant in whatever way he and the subtenant might agree. In particular, the lessor's liability could be restricted to the period while the reversion to the sublease remained vested in him. This was legally possible, if seldom met in practice. When the lessor's liability was confined in this way, and the lessor assigned the reversion, his successor would be liable under this covenant by virtue of privity of estate but the lessor's own liability by virtue of privity of contract would be at an end. The issue on this appeal is whether the 1995 Act precludes a lessor from now limiting his liability in this way. The Court of Appeal held it does: [2005] 1 WLR 236.
2.  The context is as follows. In February 2002 Avonridge Property Co Ltd acquired by assignment a lease of seven small shop units at Wealdstone, Middlesex. The lease was for a term of 99 years expiring in 2067, at an annual rent of £16,700 subject to review. Avonridge granted subleases of six of these shops for substantially the same term as its own lease, or head lease as the lease then became. The rent payable under each sublease was a peppercorn. The sublessees paid Avonridge substantial premiums for their subleases, of the order of £75,000 for each sublease.

3.  Each sublease contained, in clause 6, a landlord's covenant for quiet enjoyment and for payment of the rent reserved by the head lease. The words of covenant read as follows (commas have been added to assist reading):

    'The Landlord covenants with the Tenant as follows (but not, in the case of Avonridge Property Company Limited only, so as to be liable after the Landlord has disposed of its interest in the Property) ... .'

4.  On 2 April 2002 Avonridge assigned the head lease to a Mr Dhirajlal Phithwa. Mr Phithwa was, to use the old legal phrase, a man of straw. He disappeared, leaving unpaid the rent due under the head lease. The head lessor, the London Diocesan Fund and the Parochial Church Council of Holy Trinity, Wealdstone, commenced forfeiture proceedings. The subtenants were granted relief, on unexceptional terms: they had to pay the rent arrears under the head lease with interest and costs and take new leases of their individual units. The new leases were for the same term as their former subleases and at a rent equal to an apportioned part of the rental payable under the forfeited head lease. This meant that for the future, under the new leases, the former subtenants had to pay an annual rent of £2,376 or, in one instance, £2,441. This is to be contrasted with the nominal rent payable under the subleases they had bought from Avonridge.

5.  The subtenants brought proceedings against Avonridge, claiming damages for breach of the landlord's covenant in clause 6 of their leases. Judge Copley sitting in Willesden County Court gave judgment for the subtenants, for damages to be assessed. He held that the 1995 Act rendered void the words in clause 6 limiting Avonridge's liability to the time it was the landlord. The Court of Appeal, comprising Pill, Jonathan Parker and Hooper LJJ, dismissed Avonridge's appeal. Avonridge has now appealed to your Lordships' House.

## A trap for the unwary?

6.  It must be said at once that Avonridge's case is not overburdened with merit. Indeed, on their face the transactions have the appearance of a scam. The sublessees' security, and the value of their subleases, depended on the strength of the sublessor's covenant to pay the head lease rental. But Avonridge could end its liability to pay this rent at any time. There was, it seems, no restriction on assignment of the head lease. If Avonridge assigned the head lease its liability as tenant of that lease would end automatically, by virtue of section 5 of the 1995 Act. Its liability as landlord under the subleases would also end automatically, by virtue of the limited terms of the landlord's covenant in clause 6 of the subleases.

7.  An assignee of the head lease from Avonridge would, of course, become liable to the head lessor in respect of the tenant's covenants in the head lease. An assignee would also become liable to the sublessees in respect of the landlord's covenant in clause 6 of the subleases. In each instance this liability would arise by virtue of privity of estate. But no one of financial substance would take an assignment of the head lease and thereby incur liability to pay rent of £16,700 per annum to the head lessor, save on payment of a substantial 'reverse' premium. No one would do so, because the property for which this rent was payable was let on correspondingly long subleases yielding no rental income.

8.  Thus the overall position was that Avonridge received premiums from the subtenants totalling altogether £458,500 in exchange for subleases which from their inception were essentially valueless. They were valueless because by its own act of assignment to a worthless assignee Avonridge could at any time put the subleases in jeopardy of forfeiture. Avonridge could do this without incurring any liability either to the head lessor or to the subtenants. From the outset it was in

Avonridge's financial interest to take this course as soon as possible. Avonridge lost no time in doing so.

9.  How these unfortunate sublessees came to acquire and pay for these subleases is not a matter before your Lordships. Nor is the question whether any of the circumstances surrounding these transactions may afford the sublessees redress, whether against Avonridge or others. Your Lordships' House is concerned only with the rights and obligations of the parties under the terms of the subleases they entered into. But the potential use of the provisions of the 1995 Act in the manner illustrated by the facts of this case is a matter to be taken into account when interpreting the statutory provisions.

## The 1995 Act

10. The 1995 Act gave effect, with amendments, to the recommendations of the Law Commission in its report 'Landlord and Tenant Law — Privity of Contract and Estate': Law Com No 174 (1988). One of the principal mischiefs the Act was intended to remedy was that, as the law stood, the original tenant of a lease remained liable for performance of the tenant's covenants throughout the entire duration of the lease. A tenant might part with his lease and many years later find himself liable for substantial amounts of unpaid rent, perhaps much increased under rent review provisions, and for the cost of making good extensive dilapidations.

11. This was considered unfair. This potential liability was not widely understood by tenants, and it could lead to hardship. Section 5 of the Act remedied this defect in the law. Section 5 provides that where a tenant assigns the whole of the premises demised to him under a tenancy, he is released from the tenant covenants of the tenancy. A tenant covenant is a covenant falling to be complied with by the tenant of premises demised by the tenancy. Tenancy includes a sub-tenancy: section 28(1).

12. Section 6 contains a corresponding provision for the benefit of landlords in respect of landlord covenants, but this provision is not so far-reaching in its effect. Unlike the automatic release of tenant covenants brought about by assignment of the whole of the demised premises, assignment of the reversion in the whole of the demised premises does not automatically relieve the landlord from his liability under the landlord covenants. The Law Commission considered the new provision regarding landlord covenants could not precisely mirror the position regarding tenant covenants. Tenants rarely, if ever, have a right to give or withhold consent to dispositions by their landlord. Moreover, there was less need for radical change with landlord covenants because landlords undertake far fewer obligations than tenants, and landlords may not be troubled by the prospect of continuing responsibility: see para 4.16 of its report.

13. So sections 6 to 8 of the Act provide a landlord with a means which may result in his being released from the landlord covenants but will not necessarily do so. If the landlord assigns the whole of the premises of which he is landlord, he may apply to be released from the landlord covenants of the tenancy. A landlord covenant is a covenant falling to be complied with by the landlord of the premises demised by a tenancy. An application for release is made by the landlord serving an appropriate notice on the tenant requesting a release of the landlord covenant wholly or in part. Where the landlord makes such an application the covenant is released to the requested extent if the tenant consents, or if he fails to object, or if he does object but the court decides it is reasonable for the covenant to be released: section 8.

14. These statutory provisions might readily be stultified if the parties to a lease could exclude their operation. In particular, the provision for automatic release of tenant covenants on assignment of a lease would be a weak instrument if it were open to a landlord to provide that the original tenant's contractual liability should continue

for the whole term notwithstanding section 5. So the Act, in section 25, enacts a comprehensive anti-avoidance provision. Subsection (1) relevantly provides:

'Any agreement relating to a tenancy is void to the extent that—

(a) it would apart from this section have effect to exclude, modify or otherwise frustrate the operation of any provision of this Act, or

(b) it provides for—

(i) the termination or surrender of the tenancy, or

(ii) the imposition on the tenant of any penalty, disability, or liability,

in the event of the operation of any provision of this Act ...'

The words in parenthesis in Avonridge's covenant in clause 6 of each sublease are an 'agreement relating to a tenancy' within the meaning of this section: section 25(4). But does this agreement 'frustrate the operation' of any provision of the Act? That is the key question.

15. The subtenants submit it does. The limited release provisions in sections 6 to 8 were intended to be the sole means whereby an original landlord could obtain a release from the landlord covenants when he assigned the reversion. The parenthetical words in clause 6 would frustrate that statutory purpose if they were allowed to have effect according to their tenor.

16. I am unable to agree. Where I part company with this submission is its statement of the statutory purpose. Sections 5 to 8 are relieving provisions. They are intended to benefit tenants, or landlords, as the case may be. That is their purpose. That is how they are meant to operate. These sections introduced a means, which cannot be ousted, whereby in certain circumstances, without the agreement of the other party, a tenant or landlord can be released from a liability he has assumed. The object of the legislation was that on lawful assignment of a tenancy or reversion, and irrespective of the terms of the tenancy, the tenant or the landlord should have an exit route from his future liabilities. This route should be available in accordance with the statutory provisions.

17. Thus the mischief at which the statute was aimed was the absence in practice of any such exit route. Consistently with this the legislation was not intended to close any other exit route already open to the parties: in particular, that by agreement their liability could be curtailed from the outset or later released or waived. The possibility that by agreement the parties may limit their liability in this way was not, it seems, perceived as having unfair consequences in practice, even though landlords normally have greater bargaining power than tenants. So, there was no call for legislation to exclude the parties' capacity to make such an agreement, ending their liability in circumstances other than those provided in the Act.

18. Section 25 is, of course, to be interpreted generously, so as to ensure the operation of the Act is not frustrated, either directly or indirectly. But there is nothing in the language or scheme of the Act to suggest the statute was intended to exclude the parties' ability to limit liability under their covenants from the outset in whatever way they may agree. An agreed limitation of this nature does not impinge upon the operation of the statutory provisions.

19. This is so whether the agreed limitation is included in the lease itself or is in a separate document by way of waiver or agreement to release. The legal effect is the same in each case. Whatever its form, an agreed limitation of liability does not impinge upon the operation of the statutory provisions because, as already noted, the statutory provisions are intended to operate to relieve tenants and landlords from a liability which would otherwise exist. They are not intended to impose a liability which otherwise would be absent. They are not intended to enlarge the liability either of a tenant or landlord. The Act does not compel a landlord to enter into a covenant with his tenant to pay the rent under a head lease. The Act does not compel this, even though it may be eminently reasonable that a landlord should do so. Nor do the statutory restrictions on the circumstances where a landlord can end his liability without his tenant's consent carry any implication

that a tenant may not agree to end his landlord's liability in other circumstances. Such an implication would be inconsistent with the underlying scheme of these provisions.

20. This appraisal accords with the thrust of the Law Commission's report. The commission expressly recognised, in paragraph 2.17, that the parties to a lease were able to limit their obligations so that their obligations ended on disposal of their interests:

> A lease can, as a matter of bargain, limit the obligations of one or both of the parties, so that they come to an end if the parties transfer their interest in the property. However, this is rarely done.

A similar view is expressed in paragraph 3.3: the continuing liability of the original parties to leases is a 'matter of contract'. The parties 'are free to vary the normal rule'. This is 'sometimes done, but not frequently'. Nowhere in its report does the commission suggest the parties' freedom to vary the normal rule has given rise to problems and should be curtailed. Had such a fundamental incursion into basic law been intended that would surely have found clear expression in the Act.

21. Nor do the events in this case exemplify a loophole in the Act Parliament cannot have intended. The risks involved were not obscure or concealed. They were evident on the face of the subleases. The sublessees were to pay up-front a capitalised rent for the whole term of the subleases. But clause 6 enabled Avonridge to shake off all its landlord obligations at will. Any competent conveyancer would, or should, have warned the sublessees of the risks, clearly and forcefully ...

40. It would, of course, have been open to Parliament, when passing the 1995 Act, to limit the initial landlord's freedom to contract out of any continuing liability. But there is nothing in the 1995 Act which effects such a fundamental change of principle. Given the concerns of the property industry which led to the modifications of the Law Commission's recommendations, it would have been surprising if there were. The provisions with which we are concerned, principally sections 6 and 8 of the 1995 Act, are closely modelled on those in clauses 4 and 6 of the Bill annexed to the Law Commission's Report (allowing for the stylistic changes which often seem to take place when a new draftsman takes over another's draft). I cannot find in them, or in section 3, which is concerned to identify those covenants which fall within the doctrine of privity of estate and are thus *capable* of running with the tenancy and the reversion, anything to suggest such a radical change in policy.

\* \* \*

**Source 2**

### *Jervis v Harris* [1996] Ch 195

In the Action the Plaintiff landlord seeks to enforce certain covenants contained in an underlease dated 11th July 1947 for a term of 999 years less 10 days from 24th December 1899.

The first of the preliminary issues ('the Construction Issue') concerns the true construction of the tenant's repairing covenant contained in Clause 2(7) of the underlease. The second and third preliminary issues are concerned with Clause 2(10) of the underlease which gives the landlord the right from time to time during the term to enter on the demised premises to view the state of repair and to remedy any want of repair at the tenant's expense. The second preliminary issue ('the 1938 Act Issue') is whether the Clause is enforceable by the landlord without the leave of the Court first obtained under Section 1 of the Leasehold Property (Repairs) Act 1938. The third preliminary issue ('the Penalty Issue') is whether the moneys due by way of reimbursement to the landlord pursuant to the Clause are irrecoverable as a penalty.

## 1    The Construction Issue

Clause 2(7) of the underlease is in the following terms.

> the lessees will at all times during the said term maintain, repair, and keep in good tenantable repair and condition in all respects whatsoever the buildings which now are, or shall hereafter be, erected or standing upon the said premises and their respective appurtenances and will, when necessary, rebuild the said buildings, or any of them, so that they may be at all times during the said term of the clear letting value of £1,000 per annum.

The issue is framed as follows:

> Whether or not on the true and proper construction of clause 2(7) of the lease the repairing liability thereunder of the defendant only obliges the defendant to carry out such works of repair, if any, as may be necessary to ensure that the clear letting value of the demise premises and the buildings thereon at all times during the term of 999 years less the last 10 days thereof granted by the lease is £80 per annum or is alternatively £1,000 per annum.

The Judge answered the question in the negative.

The Judge held that they qualify the second obligation only. He reached his conclusion for two reasons. First, the standard to which the obligation to repair is to be performed is expressed in the Clause as 'in good tenantable repair and condition'. That standard is not by any means necessarily the same as sufficient to secure a letting value of £1,000 per annum. Neither could sensibly stand as a proviso to the other. Secondly, it was necessary to specify the event on the occasion of which the obligation to rebuild should arise, and this was achieved by the concluding words of the Clause. Accordingly, the Judge read these words as indicating both when the obligation to rebuild arose and also the standard to which, or the nature of the new building which, it was the obligation of the tenant to carry out. Accordingly, the Judge declared that the concluding words of the Clause qualified the second or rebuilding obligation but not the first or repairing obligation.

## 2    The 1938 Act Issue

Clause 2(10) of the underlease authorises the landlord or the superior landlords to enter upon the demised premises from time to time during the term granted to view the state of repair and to give notice in writing to the tenant of any defects or want of repair. The tenant is required within three months to make good all such defects or want of repair of which he has been given notice, and in default the landlord or the superior landlords may do the work themselves and recover the costs and expenses of the work from the tenant on demand.

The Plaintiff has caused the premises to be inspected and has served a notice specifying the wants of repair which he alleges exist on the property. The Defendant has failed to carry out any of the work needed to remedy such wants of repair, and it is the landlord's intention to exercise his rights under Clause 2(10) of the underlease to enter and do the work himself and recover the cost from the Defendant. The Defendant has refused to allow the Plaintiff or his workmen to enter upon the premises, and the Plaintiff has accordingly brought the present proceedings seeking inter alia an injunction to restrain the Defendant from preventing him from entering the premises and carrying out works of repair thereon.

The short answer to the question is that the tenant's liability to reimburse the landlord for his expenditure on repairs is not a liability in damages for breach of his repairing covenant all. The landlord's claim sounds in debt not damages; and it is not a claim to compensation for breach of the tenant's covenant to repair, but for reimbursement of sums actually spent by the landlord in carrying out repairs himself.

Leaving aside for the moment the landlord's claim to reimbursement, his contractual right to enter the property and effect the repairs himself if the tenant does not do so is plainly outside the Section. Nothing in the Section requires him to obtain the leave of the Court either before entry or before service of notice of disrepair. Should he then decide to bring proceedings for forfeiture or damages for breach of covenant, whether to repair or to repair on notice, he must first obtain the leave of the Court under the Section. But if he chooses instead to effect the repairs himself, there is nothing in the Section which requires him to obtain the leave of the Court before doing so. So the question is: does the Section require him to obtain the leave of the Court after having carried out the repairs and before demanding reimbursement? But this claim cannot sensibly be described as a claim to damages for breach of the tenant's repairing covenant. That breach has been remedied. The landlord sues in re-spect of an altogether different breach which occurs when the tenant fails to repay the landlord on demand the amount which he promised to pay.

**Order: Appeal dismissed. Defendant to pay the plaintiff's costs of the appeal, not to be enforced without the leave of the Court.**

*   *   *

**Source 3**

Contains public sector information licensed under the Open Government Licence v3.0.

## Landlord and Tenant Act 1927

### 18   Provisions as to covenants to repair

(1) Damages for a breach of a covenant or agreement to keep or put premises in repair during the currency of a lease, or to leave or put premises in repair at the termination of a lease, whether such covenant or agreement is expressed or implied, and whether general or specific, shall in no case exceed the amount (if any) by which the value of the reversion (whether immediate or not) in the premises is diminished owing to the breach of such covenant or agreement as aforesaid; and in particular no damage shall be recovered for a breach of any such covenant or agreement to leave or put premises in repair at the termination of a lease, if it is shown that the premises, in whatever state of repair they might be, would at or shortly after the termination of the tenancy have been or be pulled

down, or such structural alterations made therein as would render valueless the repairs covered by the covenant or agreement.

(2) A right of re-entry or forfeiture for a breach of any such covenant or agreement as aforesaid shall not be enforceable, by action or otherwise, unless the lessor proves that the fact that such a notice as is required by section one hundred and forty-six of the Law of Property Act, 1925, had been served on the lessee was known either—

(a) to the lessee; or

(b) to an under-lessee holding under an under-lease which reserved a nominal reversion only to the lessee; or

(c) to the person who last paid the rent due under the lease either on his own behalf or as agent for the lessee or under-lessee;

and that a time reasonably sufficient to enable the repairs to be executed had elapsed since the time when the fact of the service of the notice came to the knowledge of any such person.

Where a notice has been sent by registered post, addressed to a person at his last known place of abode in the United Kingdom, then, for the purposes of this subsection, that person shall be deemed, unless the contrary is proved, to have had knowledge of the fact that the notice had been served as from the time at which the letter would have been delivered in the ordinary course of post.

This subsection shall be construed as one with section one hundred and forty-six of the Law of Property Act, 1925.

(3) This section applies whether the lease was created before or after the commencement of this Act.

\* \* \*

**Source 4**

Contains public sector information licensed under the Open Government Licence v3.0.

# Landlord and Tenant (Covenants) Act 1995

### 3   Transmission of benefit and burden of covenants

(1) The benefit and burden of all landlord and tenant covenants of a tenancy—

(a) shall be annexed and incident to the whole, and to each and every part, of the premises demised by the tenancy and of the reversion in them, and

(b) shall in accordance with this section pass on an assignment of the whole or any part of those premises or of the reversion in them.

(2) Where the assignment is by the tenant under the tenancy, then as from the assignment the assignee—

(a)   becomes bound by the tenant covenants of the tenancy except to the extent that—

(i)  immediately before the assignment they did not bind the assignor, or

(ii) they fall to be complied with in relation to any demised premises not comprised in the assignment; and

(b) becomes entitled to the benefit of the landlord covenants of the tenancy except to the extent that they fall to be complied with in relation to any such premises.

(3) Where the assignment is by the landlord under the tenancy, then as from the assignment the assignee—
  (a) becomes bound by the landlord covenants of the tenancy except to the extent that—
     (i) immediately before the assignment they did not bind the assignor, or
     (ii) they fall to be complied with in relation to any demised premises not comprised in the assignment; and
  (b) becomes entitled to the benefit of the tenant covenants of the tenancy except to the extent that they fall to be complied with in relation to any such premises.
(4) In determining for the purposes of subsection (2) or (3) whether any covenant bound the assignor immediately before the assignment, any waiver or release of the covenant which (in whatever terms) is expressed to be personal to the assignor shall be disregarded.
(5) Any landlord or tenant covenant of a tenancy which is restrictive of the user of land shall, as well as being capable of enforcement against an assignee, be capable of being enforced against any other person who is the owner or occupier of any demised premises to which the covenant relates, even though there is no express provision in the tenancy to that effect.
(6) Nothing in this section shall operate—
  (a) in the case of a covenant which (in whatever terms) is expressed to be personal to any person, to make the covenant enforceable by or (as the case may be) against any other person; or
  (b) to make a covenant enforceable against any person if, apart from this section, it would not be enforceable against him by reason of its not having been registered under the [Land Registration Act 2002] or the Land Charges Act 1972.
(7) To the extent that there remains in force any rule of law by virtue of which the burden of a covenant whose subject matter is not in existence at the time when it is made does not run with the land affected unless the covenantor covenants on behalf of himself and his assigns, that rule of law is hereby abolished in relation to tenancies.

\* \* \*

**Source 5**

Contains public sector information licensed under the Open Government Licence v3.0.

# Law of Property Act 1925

### 146 Restrictions on and relief against forfeiture of leases and underleases

(1) A right of re-entry or forfeiture under any proviso or stipulation in a lease for a breach of any covenant or condition in the lease shall not be enforceable, by action or otherwise, unless and until the lessor serves on the lessee a notice—
  (a) specifying the particular breach complained of; and
  (b) if the breach is capable of remedy, requiring the lessee to remedy the breach; and
  (c) in any case, requiring the lessee to make compensation in money for the breach.
  and the lessee fails, within a reasonable time thereafter, to remedy the breach, if it is capable of remedy, and to make reasonable compensation in money, to the satisfaction of the lessor, for the breach.

(2) Where a lessor is proceeding, by action or otherwise, to enforce such a right of re-entry or forfeiture, the lessee may, in the lessor's action, if any, or in any action brought by himself, apply to the court for relief; and the court may grant or refuse relief, as the court, having regard to the proceedings and conduct of the parties under the foregoing provisions of this section, and to all the other circumstances, thinks fit; and in case of relief may grant it on such terms, if any, as to costs, expenses, damages, compensation, penalty, or otherwise, including the granting of an injunction to restrain any like breach in the future, as the court, in the circumstances of each case, thinks fit.

(3) A lessor shall be entitled to recover as a debt due to him from a lessee, and in addition to damages (if any), all reasonable costs and expenses properly incurred by the lessor in the employment of a solicitor and surveyor or valuer, or otherwise, in reference to any breach giving rise to a right of re-entry or forfeiture which, at the request of the lessee, is waived by the lessor, or from which the lessee is relieved, under the provisions of this Act.

(4) Where a lessor is proceeding by action or otherwise to enforce a right of re-entry or forfeiture under any covenant, proviso, or stipulation in a lease, or for non-payment of rent, the court may, on application by any person claiming as under-lessee any estate or interest in the property comprised in the lease or any part thereof, either in the lessor's action (if any) or in any action brought by such person for that purpose, make an order vesting, for the whole term of the lease or any less term, the property comprised in the lease or any part thereof in any person entitled as under-lessee to any estate or interest in such property upon such conditions as to execution of any deed or other document, payment of rent, costs, expenses, damages, compensation, giving security, or otherwise, as the court in the circumstances of each case may think fit, but in no case shall any such under-lessee be entitled to require a lease to be granted to him for any longer term than he had under his original sub-lease.

(5) For the purposes of this section—

   (a) 'Lease' includes an original or derivative under-lease; also, an agreement for a lease where the lessee has become entitled to have his lease granted; also, a grant at a fee farm rent, or securing a rent by conditions.

   (b) 'Lessee' includes an original or derivative under-lessee, and the persons deriving title under a lessee; also, a grantee under any such grant as aforesaid and the persons deriving title under him.

   (c) 'Lessor' includes an original or derivative under-lessor, and the persons deriving title under a lessor; also, a person making such grant as aforesaid and the persons deriving title under him.

   (d) 'Under-lease' includes an agreement for an under-lease where the under-lessee has become entitled to have his underlease granted.

   (e) 'Under-lessee' includes any person deriving title under an under-lessee.

(6) This section applies although the proviso or stipulation under which the right of re-entry or forfeiture accrues is inserted in the lease in pursuance of the directions of any Act of Parliament.

(7) For the purposes of this section a lease limited to continue as long only as the lessee abstains from committing a breach of covenant shall be and take effect as a lease to continue for any longer term for which it could subsist, but determinable by a proviso for re-entry on such a breach.

(8) This section does not extend—

   (i) To a covenant or condition against assigning, underletting, parting with the possession, or disposing of the land leased where the breach occurred before the commencement of this Act; or

   (ii) In the case of a mining lease, to a covenant or condition for allowing the lessor to have access to or inspect books, accounts, records, weighing machines or other things, or to enter or inspect the mine or the workings thereof.

(9) This section does not apply to a condition for forfeiture on the bankruptcy of the lessee or on taking in execution of the lessee's interest if contained in a lease of—
  (a) Agricultural or pastoral land.
  (b) Mines or minerals
  (c)  A house used or intended to be used as a public-house or beershop.
  (d) A house let as a dwelling-house, with the use of any furniture, books, works of art, or other chattels not being in the nature of fixtures.
  (e)  Any property with respect to which the personal qualifications of the tenant are of importance for the preservation of the value or character of the property, or on the ground of neighbourhood to the lessor, or to any person holding under him.
(10) Where a condition of forfeiture on the bankruptcy of the lessee or on taking in execution of the lessee's interest is contained in any lease, other than a lease of any of the classes mentioned in the last sub-section, then—
  (a) if the lessee's interest is sold within one year from the bankruptcy or taking in execution, this section applies to the forfeiture condition aforesaid.
  (b) if the lessee's interest is not sold before the expiration of that year, this section only applies to the forfeiture condition aforesaid during the first year from the date of the bankruptcy or taking in execution.
(11)  This section does not, save as otherwise mentioned, affect the law relating to re-entry or forfeiture or relief in case of non-payment of rent.
(12)  This section has effect notwithstanding any stipulation to the contrary.
[F1(13)  The county court has jurisdiction under this section ...]

\* \* \*

**Source 6**

Contains public sector information licensed under the Open Government Licence v3.0.

## Leasehold Property (Repairs) Act 1938

**1    Restriction on enforcement of repairing covenants in long leases of small houses**

(1) Where a lessor serves on a lessee under subsection (1) of section one hundred and forty-six of the Law of Property Act, 1925, a notice that relates to a breach of a covenant or agreement to keep or put in repair during the currency of the lease [all or any of the property comprised in the lease], and at the date of the service of the notice [three] years or more of the term of the lease remain unexpired, the lessee may within twenty-eight days from that date serve on the lessor a counter-notice to the effect that he claims the benefit of this Act.
(2) A right to damages for a breach of such a covenant as aforesaid shall not be enforceable by action commenced at any time at which [three] years or more of the term of the lease remain unexpired unless the lessor has served on the lessee not less than one month before the commencement of the action such a notice as is specified in subsection (1) of section one hundred and forty-six of the Law of Property Act, 1925, and where a notice is served under this subsection, the lessee may, within twenty-eight days from the date of the service thereof, serve on the lessor a counter-notice to the effect that he claims the benefit of this Act.
(3) Where a counter-notice is served by a lessee under this section, then, notwithstanding anything in any enactment or rule of law, no proceedings, by action or otherwise, shall be taken by the lessor for the enforcement of any right

of re-entry or forfeiture under any proviso or stipulation in the lease for breach of the covenant or agreement in question, or for damages for breach thereof, otherwise than with the leave of the court.

(4) A notice served under subsection (1) of section one hundred and forty-six of the Law of Property Act, 1925, in the circumstances specified in subsection (1) of this section, and a notice served under subsection (2) of this section shall not be valid unless it contains a statement, in characters not less conspicuous than those used in any other part of the notice, to the effect that the lessee is entitled under this Act to serve on the lessor a counter-notice claiming the benefit of this Act, and a statement in the like characters specifying the time within which, and the manner in which, under this Act a counter-notice may be served and specifying the name and address for service of the lessor.

(5) Leave for the purposes of this section shall not be given unless the lessor proves—

(a) that the immediate remedying of the breach in question is requisite for preventing substantial diminution in the value of his reversion, or that the value thereof has been substantially diminished by the breach.

(b) that the immediate remedying of the breach is required for giving effect in relation to the [premises] to the purposes of any enactment, or of any byelaw or other provision having effect under an enactment, [or for giving effect to any order of a court or requirement of any authority under any enactment or any such byelaw or other provision as aforesaid].

(c) in a case in which the lessee is not in occupation of the whole of the [premises as respects which the covenant or agreement is proposed to be enforced], that the immediate remedying of the breach is required in the interests of the occupier of those premises] or of part thereof;

(d) that the breach can be immediately remedied at an expense that is relatively small in comparison with the much greater expense that would probably be occasioned by postponement of the necessary work; or

(e) special circumstances which in the opinion of the court, render it just and equitable that leave should be given.

(6) The court may, in granting or in refusing leave for the purposes of this section, impose such terms and conditions on the lessor or on the lessee as it may think fit.

\* \* \*

## ■ YOUR TURN

Have a go at answering question 2, remembering the guidance on pages 19–20.
- Refer to the structured approach in the SRA's assessment criteria on page 20.
- Create a list of the most important pieces of information to assist with your answer, providing relevant legal advice to your supervising solicitor.
- Timings are important: you will need to prepare and write your answer in one hour.

| SQE1 Functioning legal knowledge link |
| --- |
| Remember from chapter 8 of *Revise SQE: Property Practice* that old leases are those granted before the introduction of the Landlord and Tenant (Covenants) Act 1995 and new leases are those granted after it (ie on or after 1 January 1996). |

## EVALUATING YOUR ANSWER

When you have attempted question 2, mark it yourself against the SQE2 legal research assessment criteria. Do you think your attempt met the threshold standard?

Now compare your attempt with the following key legal points and two sample answers to question 2. A circled number indicates that commentary is provided for this part of the answer. The commentary will explain whether the sample is likely to meet the threshold SQE2 standard.

In the assessment, part or all of the sources could be relevant to the question. It is imperative that you are able to identify which sources are not relevant.

## ➡Key legal points: Question 2

In this assessment, part, or all, of the following sources are relevant to the question:

- *Jervis v Harris* [1996] Ch 195
- Landlord and Tenant (Covenants) Act 1995 s 3
- Law of Property Act 1925 s 146
- Leasehold Property (Repairs) Act 1938 s 1.

The following sources are not relevant to the question:

- *Avonridge Property Co Ltd v Mashru* [2005] UKHL 70
- Landlord and Tenant Act 1927 s 18.

**Key legal points** include the following:
- Landlord and Tenant (Covenants) Act 1995 is applicable as the lease commenced in 2005. There are a few remedies available to the landlord for breach of repairing covenant. Guillermo may be able to apply for damages under the Leasehold Property (Repairs) Act 1938. Forfeiture by serving a s 146 notice under the Law of Property Act 1925 is also an option if there is a provision in the lease for this. However, with this, there is a potential for the tenant to apply for relief from forfeiture.
- Specific performance is a discretionary equitable remedy to make the tenant remedy the breach.
- Under *Jervis v Harris*, if there is a self-help clause within the lease, it could provide for a right of re-entry and for Guillermo to serve a notice of a breach on the tenants.
- For leases that were created on or after 1 January 1996, the applicable act is the Landlord and Tenants (Covenants) Act 1995. This abolished the doctrine of privity of contracts so that original tenants and successors were no longer differentiated. This ensures that any new tenants are bound by the covenants in the lease while it is vested in them.
- The remedies available for breach of leasehold covenants can be damages, forfeiture, self-help or specific performance:
  - Damages are available under the Leasehold Property (Repairs) Act 1938 for leases that are over seven years old with a minimum of three years left to run. Intention to sue must be served on a tenant and they will then have 28 days to serve a counter-notice. It is important to take into consideration the tenant's circumstances, as a key factor here is their ability to pay. In addition to this, damages will be limited to the amount of diminution of the property.
  - Forfeiture is another remedy available under the Law of Property Act 1925. There will need to be a provision in the lease for forfeiture to be an option, and the notice will need to specify what the breach is, when it needs to be rectified (reasonable time scale) and that the tenant will need to compensate the landlord for the breach. If these requirements are not followed, it can invalidate the s 146

notice. As per the Leasehold Property (Repairs) Act 1938, it is important to inform the tenant that they have 28 days to serve a counter-notice.
- If there is a *Jervis v Harris* (self-help) clause in the lease, there may be a right for the landlord to enter the property and carry out the repairs and then recover these costs from the tenant. However, as mentioned with damages, it is important to consider the tenant's ability to satisfy this debt.
- Specific performance is a discretionary equitable remedy available to force a tenant to remedy the breach. However, if other remedies are more appropriate, courts are unlikely to make an order for specific performance.

## ■ SAMPLE ANSWER 1 TO QUESTION 2

I understand Guillermo has instructed you in relation to his current dispute with his tenants and would like advice on how he can proceed.

I have researched breaches of repairing covenants and it is evident that there has been a breach of the repairing covenant in the lease. The Landlord and Tenant (Covenants) Act 1995, s 3(1) states that the benefit and burden of all landlord and tenant covenants shall be annexed and incident to the whole of the premises and shall pass on an assignment of the premises. This means that Guillermo will be able to bring an action against the current tenants, despite them not being the original tenants on the lease. ❶

In doing so, there may be a few remedies available to Guillermo. It is important to review the lease to identify whether there is a self-help clause established in *Jervis v Harris* [1996] Ch 195. In this case, the court identified that the tenant's liability to reimburse the landlord for his expenditure on repairs was not a liability in damages for breach of his repairing covenant. The landlord's claim sounded in debt not damages; and it was not a claim to compensation for breach of the tenant's covenant to repair, but for reimbursement of sums actually spent by the landlord in carrying out the repairs himself. If there is a self-help clause, Guillermo should be able to enter the property to check the tenant's compliance with the repairing covenant and serve a notice on them for any breach. If this is not rectified, he may be able to enter the property, carry out the works and recover the cost of this from the tenant in the form of a debt. However, this will be dependent on the lease provisions, and the tenant's finances should also be considered. ❷

Guillermo could also serve a s 146 notice for forfeiture providing that there is a clause for this in the lease under the Law of Property Act 1925. If there is a provision, he will need to serve a s 146 notice on the tenant, and it must include the following:
   a. what the breach is
   b. when the breach needs to be remedied (this needs to be reasonable)
   c. that they pay compensation
   d. that they have 28 days to serve a counter-notice under the Leasehold Property (Repairs) Act 1938. ❸

This may also give rise to a claim for damages. However, consideration should be made into how realistic this will be, in relation to the tenant's finances. In addition to this, if the tenant were to serve a counter-notice, Guillermo would need evidence that the breach needs to be remedied immediately. Based on the information that Guillermo has provided, it may be possible to evidence substantial diminution of the property with the quote for repairs, alongside devaluation of the property. ❹

Finally, the courts can, on occasion, make an order for specific performance. However, it is a discretionary equitable remedy, and if the courts deem any of the other remedies more appropriate, they are unlikely to make an order for specific performance. ⑤

It is evident that a breach of a leasehold covenant has occurred, and Guillermo has a few options available. If it is unlikely that the tenant will be able to pay for the repairs, forfeiture may be more appropriate to ensure that Guillermo gains control over the property and can remedy the breaches. ⑥

## COMMENTARY

① The beginning of this paragraph clearly states the position of the client. It correctly applies the appropriate law (Landlord and Tenant (Covenants) Act 1995) by utilising the information provided in the attendance note. This evidences to the examiner that the candidate is able to apply the correct law to the client's matters in addition to identifying and using relevant sources.

② This section uses a consistent structure in identifying remedies available to the client. It uses understandable language to convey facts and information effectively. Remember that, at this point, there is not enough information to determine whether a self-help clause is in the lease. This demonstrates that while the candidate is aware of the remedies, they can also identify when they need to obtain further information.

③ This provides a clear breakdown of what needs to be included if bringing a claim for forfeiture under the Law of Property Act 1925. The candidate's legal analysis is sufficiently detailed in the context of the client's case. It is presented with clear and concise language, showing the examiner the necessary steps that need to be taken for this to be a valid notice. It also points out the risks to the client, in that the tenant could serve a counter-notice, which manages client expectations.

④ This paragraph sets out the requirements to respond to a counter-notice. It identifies the evidence to satisfy the courts that the breach would need to be remedied immediately. The candidate has identified the relevant fundamental legal principles and applied them correctly to the facts of the client's case.

⑤ While identifying a further remedy available, this paragraph manages client expectations by providing realistic advice based on the scenario. This is important because although, in theory, all remedies are available, if you do not manage client expectations and they choose this option but it is not awarded, you are likely to bring your firm into disrepute by not providing clear, client-focused advice. While it is important to provide the options, it is also important to identify which are most and least likely to succeed. This evidences to the examiner that the candidate is able to apply the law both correctly and comprehensively to the client's situation, rather than just providing a list.

⑥ This summary provides clear direction in relation to the situation. It identifies that if the tenant is unlikely to be able to pay for repairs, alternative options may be more appropriate.

### Does this answer meet the threshold?

The sample answer above selects the correct sources, identifying that this is a new lease and therefore the Landlord and Tenant (Covenants) Act 1995 is applicable. It also manages client expectations by identifying specific performance as a potential remedy, while explaining this is at the discretion of the court, and advising forfeiture as the best available option. It is therefore likely to meet the threshold standard for the SQE2 legal research assessment.

Now consider the second sample answer to question 2.

## ■ SAMPLE ANSWER 2 TO QUESTION 2

There has been a breach of the repairing covenant in the lease. However, as per the Landlord and Tenant Act 1927, Guillermo will only be able to bring an action against the original tenant on the lease. He will be able to claim for damages but it shall in no case exceed the amount (if any) by which the value of the reversion (whether immediate or not) in the premises is diminished owing to the breach of such covenant or agreement. **❶**

There are four remedies available to Guillermo. One is 'self-help', established in *Jervis v Harris* [1996] Ch 195. In this case, the court identified that the tenant's liability to reimburse the landlord for his expenditure on repairs was not a liability in damages for breach of his repairing covenant all. The landlord's claim sounded in debt not damages, and it was not a claim to compensation for breach of the tenant's covenant to repair, but for reimbursement of sums actually spent by the landlord in carrying out the repairs himself. Guillermo will be able to enter the property to carry out the works and recover the cost of this from the tenant in the form of a debt. **❷**

Guillermo could also serve a s 146 notice for forfeiture under the Law of Property Act 1925. If there is a provision, he will need to serve a s 146 notice on the tenant, and it must include the following:

1. what the breach is
2. when the breach needs to be remedied (this needs to be reasonable)
3. that they pay compensation. **❸**

We do not need to worry about relief from forfeiture as per the case of *Avonridge Property Co Ltd v Mashru*. Here the courts held that whatever its form, an agreed limitation of liability did not impinge upon the operation of the statutory provisions because the statutory provisions were intended to operate to relieve tenants and landlords from a liability which would otherwise exist. They were not intended to impose a liability which otherwise would be absent. **❹**

In addition to this, Guillermo will be entitled to recover damages for the losses that he has suffered. However, consideration should be made into how realistic this will be, in relation to the tenant's finances. **❺**

Finally, Guillermo could also bring a claim for specific performance, which would allow for him to force the tenant into completing the repairs within a reasonable time frame. **❻**

## COMMENTARY

**❶** This is incorrect. As the lease is dated 2005, the Landlord and Tenant (Covenants) Act 1995 is applicable and would enable Guillermo to bring a claim against the tenants in breach of the covenant, despite the fact that they were not the original tenants. This paragraph is misguided and does not identify the relevant law.

**❷** This paragraph is misleading and does not provide clear, appropriate advice. It fails to advise the client that there needs to be a self-help clause in the lease in addition to the requirements under *Jervis v Harris*. Instead, it advises that Guillermo could enter and initiate repairs immediately. However, he would first need to identify the repairs required and then serve notice of the breach. If the breach is not rectified within a reasonable time frame, Guillermo could then enter the property and make the repairs. It is unlikely that this response would meet the SQE2 legal research assessment criteria as although it does identify appropriate law, it does not relay this to the client in a clear and comprehensive manner.

(3) This section does not incorporate the law in a comprehensive manner. It omits the need to include a provision to notify the tenant of having 28 days to serve a counter-notice under the Leasehold Property (Repairs) Act 1938. This has the potential to provide the client with incorrect advice which could result in a professional misconduct claim against the firm. It would not satisfy the SQE2 legal research assessment criteria as it does not apply the law correctly or comprehensively to the client's situation.

(4) This paragraph is confusing to follow. The language used is archaic and it fails to explain to the partner the correct position of the client. The candidate has not applied the legal principles correctly and therefore is unlikely to satisfy the SQE2 legal research assessment criteria.

(5) While Guillermo will be entitled to bring a claim for damages against the tenants, it is important to note that this will be limited to the reduction in the value of the landlord's reversion.

(6) Although specific performance is an equitable remedy that could be available to Guillermo, remember this is at the courts' discretion and it is unlikely that they will opt for this remedy if self-help, damages or forfeiture are available. This does not manage the client's expectations, and it is unlikely to evidence to the examiner that the candidate has fully understood and applied the law correctly to the client's situation.

### Does this answer meet the threshold?

It is unlikely that this answer would meet the threshold standard for the SQE2 legal research assessment. When assessed against the SQE2 legal research assessment criteria, it does not apply the relevant law precisely, it is not clear and it has omissions that have affected the advice provided. It does not identify that this is a new lease and therefore incorrectly advises that Guillermo can only bring a claim against the original tenants. It also omits the need for there to be a self-help clause in the lease in addition to the requirements under *Jervis v Harris*, in order to carry out repairs and recover the cost of doing this.

## ■ KEY POINT CHECKLIST

This chapter has covered the following key knowledge points:

- The SQE2 legal research assessment criteria and how to apply them in the context of property practice.
- A suggested structure for approaching an SQE2 legal research assessment question.
- What remedies are available to clients (that are both likely and unlikely to meet the threshold standard) as a result of delayed completion or for breaches of leasehold covenants, with full commentary on the sample answers' strengths and weaknesses.

## ■ SUMMARY AND REFLECTION

In order to succeed in the SQE2 legal research assessment, you will need to take some time to review all the information provided in the supporting documents before beginning the task. When you have done this, jot down a brief plan for your answer, including all the legal advice that needs to be explained to a client in layman's terms.

Remember that you are being assessed on your ability to identify and use relevant sources alongside applying this to a client's problem. You will need to consider the issues, identify relevant sources and correctly apply them to the scenario using precise and acceptable language.

To prepare for this assessment, practise interpreting, evaluating and applying the results of research. When interpreting research, remember to use multiple sources of information to reach reasoned decisions, and ensure your advice is supported by appropriate sources. If your answer does not include legal reasoning, you will be penalised for this in the assessment.

Now take the time to reflect and consider what you might still need to work on, and whether you feel completely confident in your legal research skills in the context of property practice.

# 3

# Legal writing

## ■ MAKE SURE YOU KNOW

This chapter covers the skill of legal writing in the context of property law. Legal writing in property law is one of the legal skills that may be assessed on day one of the SQE2 assessments (see the Introduction for more detail). The SQE2 can test candidates' knowledge of both the processes associated with property law and the application of land law principles to these processes. It is imperative that you read this revision guide once you have familiarised yourself with the contents of **Revise SQE: Land Law** and **Revise SQE: Property Practice**. Deducing and investigating title is developed further within this book to identify the ways in which the SQE2 skills assessments incorporate the legal principles you will have learned for your SQE1 examinations.

This chapter provides examples of how to deduce and investigate title in registered land, in addition to reporting on title to clients. It identifies potential issues that need resolution prior to exchange of contracts, as well as further action required, which could arise in the context of an SQE2 legal writing assessment.

## ■ SQE ASSESSMENT ADVICE

As you work through this chapter, pay attention in your revision to:
• the documents provided to you to assist in the writing task in the sample answers
• the structure used in the letters or emails for ease of use by the reader
• the way in which the letters or emails are tailored to the recipient
• addressing all relevant legal and factual issues
• using clear, accurate and succinct language
• ensuring the law is applied correctly to the client's situation
• the way in which any ethical or professional conduct issues are identified and resolved.

See the Appendix for the SRA's performance indicators in legal writing.

## ■ INTRODUCTION TO LEGAL WRITING IN PROPERTY PRACTICE

The aim of the SQE2 assessments is to replicate scenarios from practice, so you will be required to address common legal issues in the field of property law. Property law is particularly client-facing and therefore it is essential that solicitors are able to write clearly, using appropriate terminology to ensure client understanding, and can apply the law correctly to a client's situation. The SQE2 legal writing assessment will be to write a letter or an email as the solicitor acting in a matter, which clearly and correctly applies the law within the context of property to the client's concerns. It will need to be appropriate for the recipient and, when writing to a client, your answer should avoid the use of legal jargon. You will be expected to apply the knowledge that you have developed from SQE1 to the scenario in a clear and concise manner. This chapter will provide examples of how you can do this and meet the assessment criteria for the SQE2 legal writing assessment.

To formulate a comprehensive answer to the SQE2 legal writing assessment, approach the question in a structured manner. Try adopting the following method:

1. Once you have read the question, write down the key legal and procedural points that you will need to communicate to the recipient.
2. You can then form the structure of the letter or email.
3. Write your answer, making sure you:
   - identify your audience and use appropriate terminology
   - avoid the use of legalese where possible when writing to clients
   - use headings and lists to assist the reader, where appropriate.
4. Review your answer, keeping in mind the SQE2 legal writing assessment criteria.

## Assessment technique

When investigating title, drafting requisitions on title or reporting on title to clients, it is useful to create a checklist of things to look out for (for example, ensuring the title is an up-to-date copy within six months as required by lenders; requesting copies of plans and documents referred to in the title) in addition to any other action to be taken. This is to ensure that you do not miss any information that requires further investigation, as ultimately this could lead to a professional negligence claim being made against the firm.

## SQE2 legal writing assessment criteria

Ensure that you follow these criteria when drafting your answer:

### Skills

1. Include relevant facts.
2. Use a logical structure.
3. Make sure advice/content is client- and recipient-focused.
4. Use clear, precise, concise and acceptable language which is appropriate to the recipient.

### Application of law

5. Apply the law correctly to the client's situation.
6. Apply the law comprehensively to the client's situation, identifying any ethical and professional conduct issues and exercising judgement to resolve them honestly and with integrity.

In chapter 2 of **Revise SQE: Property Practice**, we considered the deduction and investigation of title, including key issues to look out for. Question 1 below demonstrates how your knowledge of this topic could be tested in the context and format of an SQE2 legal writing assessment.

# ■ QUESTION 1

## Email to candidate

**From:** Partner
**Sent:** 29 November 202#
**To:** Candidate
**Subject:** Purchase of 39 Landsdown Avenue

I am acting on behalf of Mr Piotr Bielak and Ms Brygida Jurowski in their purchase of 39 Landsdown Avenue, from Mr Kwame Dembele. The seller only purchased the property last year but is now selling the property for £384,500.

**I would be grateful if you could review the attached office copy entries (Attachment 1) with a view to drafting requisitions on title to send to the seller's solicitors: TK Solicitors, 37 Camden Avenue, Fairfields, Milton Hill, MH1 8YD.**

Thanks

Partner

**Attachment 1**

Contains public sector information licensed under the Open Government Licence v3.0.

| Official copy of register of title | Title number L498537 | Edition date 02.08.2007 |
|---|---|---|

- This official copy shows the entries in the register of title on 24.3.202# at 19:54:33.
- This date must be quoted as the 'search from date' in any official search application based on this copy.
- The date at the beginning of an entry is the date on which the entry was made in the register.
- Issued on (24th March 202#).
- Under s. 67 of the Land Registration Act 2002, this copy is admissible in evidence to the same extent as the original.
- For more information about the register of title see Land Registry website www.landregistry.gov.uk or Land Registry Guide 1 – A guide to the information we keep and how you can obtain it.
- This title is dealt with by the Land Registry Leicester Office.

## A: Property Register
**This register describes the land and estate comprised in the Title.**

Grantshire        :        Milton Hill

1.  (24th March 202#) The freehold land shown edged with red on the plan of the above title filed at the registry and being known as 39 Landsdown Avenue, Fairfields, Milton Hill, MH11 4BM.

2.  (2nd August 2007) The land has the benefit of a right of way on foot only over the passageway to the west of the land leading to Overdown Farm, shown hatched blue on the title plan.

# B: Proprietorship Register

**This register specifies the class of title and identifies the owner. It contains any entries that affect the right of disposal.**

**Title Absolute**

1.  (24th March 202#) PROPRIETORS: Kwame Dembele and Abeni Dembele both of 39 Landsdown Avenue, Fairfields, Milton Hill, MH11 4BM.
2.  (24th March 202#) The price stated to have been paid on 7th March 202# was £213,500.
3.  (24th March 202#) RESTRICTION: No disposition by a sole proprietor of the registered estate (except a trust corporation) under which capital money arises is to be registered unless authorised by an order of the court.
4.  The Transfer to the proprietor contains a covenant to observe and perform the covenants referred to in the Charges Register and of an indemnity in respect thereof.

---

# C: Charges Register

**This register contains any charges and other matters that affect the land**

1.  (28th August 1964) A conveyance of the land in this title and other land dated 13th August 1964 made between (1) John Barton (Vendor) and (2) Laura O'Neil (Purchaser) contains the following covenant:

    'A covenant not to use the property for any purpose other than the erection and enjoyment of one private dwellinghouse only with garden and garage nor to carry on thereon any trade or business whatsoever.'

2.  (2nd August 2007) A Transfer dated 21st July 2007 made between George Parton (1) and Audrey Thornton contains restrictive covenants :
    NOTE: Copy filed
3.  (24th March 202#) REGISTERED CHARGE dated 7th March 202# to secure the moneys including the further advances therein mentioned.
4.  (24th March 202#) Proprietor(s): Regional Cirencester Bank PLC of Unit 164, 166 Midsummer Blvd, Centre, Milton Hill, MH9 3BA.

**END OF REGISTER**

\* \* \*

# ■ YOUR TURN

Have a go at answering question 1, remembering the guidance on pages 55–56:
*   Refer to the structured approach in the SRA's assessment criteria on page 56.
*   Create a list of the most important pieces of information to assist you with writing to the other side's solicitor raising requisitions on title.
*   Timings are important: you will need to prepare and write your answer in 30 minutes.

| **SQE1 Functioning legal knowledge link** |
| --- |
| Remember from chapter 2 of *Revise SQE: Property Practice* that official copy entries must be less than six months old, in line with the Law Societies Conveyancing Protocol. |

## EVALUATING YOUR ANSWER

When you have attempted question 1, mark it yourself against the SQE2 legal writing assessment criteria. Do you think your attempt met the threshold standard? Reflect on any improvements that you could make.

Now compare your attempt with the following key legal points and two sample answers to question 1. A circled number indicates that commentary is provided for this part of the answer. The commentary will explain whether the sample is likely to meet the threshold SQE2 standard.

---

### ➡ Key legal points: Question 1

- You will always need sight of a plan to send to your clients, to ensure the boundary lines are correct and tally with what they have seen when viewing the property (as it is not common for solicitors to view properties in person).
- When raising requisitions, it is important to be as specific as possible. When requesting an undertaking to discharge a charge, be specific as to the date of the charge and who it is in favour of. You should not exchange contracts until the seller's solicitor has provided you with an undertaking for this. The reason for this is that you may be acting on behalf of a client and lender. The lender will usually require a first legal charge on the property being purchased. Without this undertaking from the seller's solicitors, if the charge is not removed on completion, the client lender may bring a claim for professional negligence against the firm for failing to obtain an undertaking from the seller's solicitors to remove the first legal charge.
- If there are any discrepancies, such as one party selling but two legal owners on the title, it is prudent to identify whether they hold the equitable title as joint tenants or tenants in common. To do this, look for a Form A restriction in Part B of the title, the Proprietorship Register. If there is no Form A restriction, this will likely mean that they are joint tenants and therefore, if a legal owner is deceased, a death certificate (certified) will be sufficient for land registration purposes. If there is a Form A restriction, the seller's solicitor will need to either appoint a second trustee to overreach any beneficial interests or provide a grant of representation and assent to evidence the devolution of the beneficial interest.

---

# ■ SAMPLE ANSWER 1 TO QUESTION 1

*[The law firm's address and contact details]*

TK Solicitors
37 Camden Avenue
Fairfields
Milton Hill
MH1 8YD

7 December 202#

Dear Sirs,

**Purchase of 39 Landsdown Avenue ('the Property'), Subject to Contract**

Thank you for your letter dated 29 November. Having perused the office copy entries, please see the below requisitions on title:

1.  Please provide a copy of the title plan referred to in the official copy entries of title number L498537. ❶
2.  Please provide further information in relation to the right of way over the passageway, in particular who has access to it, who is responsible for its maintenance and how frequently it is used. ❷
3.  We note that there are two legal owners registered on the title. Please confirm the reason for Kwame Dembele selling alone.
4.  We note that there is a Form A restriction on the title. If Abedi Dembele is deceased, please confirm that you will appoint a second trustee to overreach any beneficial interests. Alternatively, please provide a copy of the grant of representation and assent. ❸
5.  We note that the property price has increased significantly. Please advise the reasoning for this. ❹
6.  Please confirm whether your client has complied with the covenants referred to in clauses 1 and 2 of the charges register under Title Number L498537. Failing this, we will require an indemnity policy to be taken out at the seller's expense. ❺
7.  Please provide a copy of the Transfer dated 21 July 2017. ❻
8.  Please confirm that you undertake to discharge the charge dated 7 March 202# in favour of Regional Cirencester Bank PLC on or before completion. ❼
9.  Please provide an up-to-date copy of the title. ❽

We look forward to hearing from you in due course.

Yours faithfully,

Trainee Solicitor

## COMMENTARY

❶ This letter is written in a professional manner. It communicates the reason for the letter and sets each question as a numbered bullet point to allow for an easy-to-read, structured reply. A copy of the plan is required to allow the client to confirm the boundaries, in addition to identifying the blue hatching that has the burden of a right of way (easement) over it.

❷ This section uses a logical structure following the next point in the title. It is important to identify who has the benefit of this easement, how frequently it is used and who contributes towards the maintenance and upkeep of it. This is to ensure that the buyer clients have the full information to then decide whether they are happy with this. Remember that, at this point, either party can withdraw from the transaction. However, once exchange of contracts has taken place, they will be bound by this easement.

**3** It is clear that the legal owners held the property as tenants in common. It is therefore necessary for the seller's solicitors to appoint a second trustee or provide a grant of representation and assent to evidence the devolution of title. Without this, it will cause problems and delays when registering the buyers as the new legal owners, because the Land Registry will not update the register until they have evidence of this. Points 3 and 4 of this answer apply the law correctly, to the individual title.

**4** The length of time in conjunction with the purchase price should always be considered. In this case, the property appears to have increased significantly in value in a short space of time. There could be a potential problem which requires clarification. This is also a potential professional conduct point as you are likely to be acting on behalf of the lender and client, and therefore it is prudent to identify the reason for the increase. It could be that the market value has increased rapidly, or the seller has made significant renovations which may have required planning permission or building regulations consent. Raising this requisition will assist with further searches and enquiries.

**5** This paragraph is clear, concise and recipient-focused. It uses appropriate legalese that the solicitor will understand and respond to accordingly. It also clearly sets out expectations/resolutions if there has been a breach, which demonstrates to the examiner that the candidate can apply the law comprehensively to a client's situation. A buyer's solicitor should always ask for confirmation that no covenant has been breached. If there has been a breach of covenant, or the sellers are unable to confirm that they have not been breached, the seller should be asked to take out an indemnity policy at their own expense. This is because restrictive covenants run with the land. As you will note from the title, there is an indemnity covenant at number 4 of the proprietorship register. This means that the seller will probably include an indemnity covenant in the transfer (TR1) to the buyer, requiring the buyer to enter into an indemnity covenant. This means that they will then be liable for a potential breach that they were not aware of. An indemnity insurance policy will protect to some extent, because if a claim is made by a party with the benefit of the restrictive covenant, the indemnity policy will cover the losses sustained by the buyer for the breach that they were unaware of. This is also applicable with missing documents containing covenants. If the seller's solicitor is unable to provide a copy of a document referred to on the title as containing restrictive covenants, an indemnity insurance policy should be requested to be taken out at the seller's expense.

**6** This requisition is clear and specific. It directs the recipient to a specific dated document to allow them to request a copy from the Land Registry. It is important to request all documents referred to in the office copy entries. With registered land, buyers are bound by rights and interests that are included in the title (remember the mirror principle: you are not required to look behind the curtain in equity, and instead you are bound by what is in plain sight on the title). This includes burdens such as restrictive covenants, preventing future owners from doing something on the land. If these additional documents (such as transfers and conveyances) are referred to on the register, the buyer will be bound by these restrictions (*Caveat emptor* / Buyer beware). If a firm has not requested sight of these documents and the client goes ahead with the purchase, and there is a restriction preventing them from using the land in the way that they had originally planned, it will be the solicitor firm acting on behalf of the purchaser who may be liable for professional negligence for failing to make adequate investigation of title.

**7** This requisition is also clear and specific, exercising judgement in drafting appropriate wording to ensure a specific undertaking is provided by the seller's solicitor. This evidences to the examiner that the candidate understands the legal importance of undertakings being specific and measurable. It directs the recipient to a specific dated document to allow them to confirm it will be discharged on or before completion. It is important to ensure that undertakings are provided by the seller's solicitor on or before completion. This is because the buyer's lender will want to secure a first legal charge over the property if the buyers stop making their mortgage payments. If you do not secure an undertaking, there is a risk that this will not be discharged, and without an undertaking, the firm could be liable for professional negligence. If you have a specific and measurable undertaking from the seller's solicitors and the mortgage is not discharged, the burden will land on them for not complying with the undertaking (for which proceedings can be brought to enforce it).

**8** The official copy of title is over six months old. As the candidate is acting on behalf of a lender, they will need to obtain an up-to-date copy to ensure that nothing has been changed on the title.

## Does this answer meet the threshold?

The sample answer above includes all the components that require further information prior to exchange of contracts taking place. It identifies the need to obtain an undertaking from the seller's solicitor to ensure that the client's lender will have first legal charge on the property. This is particularly important when you are acting on behalf of the client and the lender as you are required to act in the best interests of both parties. In addition to this, the answer correctly identifies the need for indemnity insurance for any non-compliance of the covenants. It is therefore likely to meet the threshold standard for the SQE2 legal writing assessment.

Now consider the second sample answer to question 1.

## ■ SAMPLE ANSWER 2 TO QUESTION 1

[*The law firm's address and contact details*]

TK Solicitors
37 Camden Avenue
Fairfields
Milton Hill
MH1 8YD

7 December 202#

Dear Sirs,

**Purchase for Mr Piotr Bielak and Ms Brygida Jurowski, ('the Property') Subject to Contract 1**

We have the following questions: **2**

1. Please provide a copy of the title referred to in the official copy entries. **3**
2. We need evidence to show that Abedi Dembele is an owner and if so, why is she not in the documents. **4**
3. Why is the property worth £384,500? **5**
4. Please confirm if any covenants have been breached in the title.
5. Please provide a copy of the Transfer.
6. Please confirm that you undertake to discharge the charge on or before completion. **6**

We look forward to hearing from you in due course.

Yours sincerely, **7**

Trainee Solicitor

## COMMENTARY

① Without the property address, reference or seller's name, it may be very difficult for the seller's solicitors to identify which file these requisitions on title relate to. This heading is not professional and could result in a delay to the clients being ready for exchange.

② This letter opens poorly; there is no clear guidance as to what the questions relate to (ie the letter that they previously sent). It is unlikely that this would meet the SQE2 legal writing assessment criteria as it does not follow a logical structure.

③ This is unprofessional and needs to be proofread. As it currently reads, the candidate is requesting a copy of the title which they already have – the document being used to raise requisitions on title. What the candidate should request is a copy of the title plan. It is extremely important to request this, not only to show the boundaries but also to ensure that the blue hatching in relation to the easement is clear.

④ This enquiry is poorly written. It is unclear as to what the trainee solicitor is asking. In addition to this, it does not make sense as Abedi is the legal owner (she is listed as a legal owner on the title documentation). Each enquiry raised needs to be precise and clear in accordance with the SQE2 legal writing assessment criteria.

⑤ It is important to identify the reasons for the increase in purchase price as it may be that building regulations consent or planning permission are required. However, the sentence structure of this enquiry is unprofessional and, without providing an explanation, may seem irrelevant to the seller's solicitor. If they then fail to provide a response and the matter is delayed due to a poorly worded question, this may in turn irritate the client.

⑥ When requesting documentation referred to in the title, it is of the utmost importance that the letter clearly identifies which document is being referred to. It is insufficient to simply state 'Transfer' as there could be more than one document that needs to be requested. This is also applicable in relation to requesting undertakings. Undertakings need to be specific and measurable. If a vague undertaking is requested, the seller's solicitor will not agree to it.

⑦ Ensure that you use the correct salutation. In relation to professional letters, it is appropriate to use 'Yours faithfully'. 'Yours sincerely' would be more appropriate when addressing a client.

### Does this answer meet the threshold?

It is unlikely that this letter to the seller's solicitor would meet the threshold standard for the SQE2 legal writing assessment. It fails to request a copy of the title plan, which could result in serious consequences such as the property's marketability. A plan is always required to check that boundaries are consistent with both the client's and lender's expectations. In addition to this, it shows a lack of understanding in relation to asking for evidence of legal ownership as the title itself is the evidence of this. When assessed against the SQE2 legal writing assessment criteria, the answer is not precise, it does not follow a logical structure and it is not tailored to an appropriate professional level.

Below is a different example, writing to a client rather than a solicitor, which could also arise in the context of the SQE2 legal writing assessment.

## ■ QUESTION 2

### Email to candidate

**From:** Partner
**Sent:** 15 November 202#
**To:** Candidate
**Subject:** Purchase of 98 Farnol Road, Shard Oak, Brilindon, BR3 1XD

I am acting on behalf of Mr Mark Conway and Mrs Sue Conway who are purchasing 98 Farnol Road in Shard Oak, a detached, freehold property. I have previously received the office copy entries and raised requisitions on title with the seller's solicitor. I have now received replies to these requisitions and need to provide a report to the clients on the title.

From memory, the clients are planning to build a bungalow at the bottom of the garden for Sue's mother, so please make sure to advise accordingly.

They are currently living in rented accommodation and their correspondence address is 55a Benedict Way, Castle Green, Brilindon, BR2 2EG.

I have already discussed Joint Tenants/Tenants in Common with Mark and Sue, and they have decided to hold as Joint Tenants.

**I would be grateful if you could read the enclosed office copy entries (Attachment 1) and replies to requisitions (Attachment 2) with a view to drafting the report on title to the clients.**

Thanks

Partner

### Attachment 1

Contains public sector information licensed under the Open Government Licence v3.0.

| Official copy of register of title | Title number W4669433 | Edition date 15.03.1999 |
| --- | --- | --- |

- This official copy shows the entries in the register of title on 05.01.202# at 06:49:11.
- This date must be quoted as the 'search from date' in any official search application based on this copy.
- The date at the beginning of an entry is the date on which the entry was made in the register.
- Issued on (5th January 202#).
- Under s.67 of the Land Registration Act 2002, this copy is admissible in evidence to the same extent as the original.
- For more information about the register of title see Land Registry website www.landregistry.gov.uk or Land Registry Guide 1 – *A guide to the information we keep and how you can obtain it.*
- This title is dealt with by the Land Registry Westenry Office.

## A: Property Register
**This register describes the land and estate comprised in the Title.**

North Midlands            :            Westenry

1.  (27th August 202#) The freehold land shown edged with red on the plan of the above title filed at the registry and being known as 98 Farnol Road, Shard Oak, Brilindon, BR3 1XD.

## B: Proprietorship Register
**This register specifies the class of title and identifies the owner. It contains any entries that affect the right of disposal.**

**Title Absolute**
1.  (27th August 202#) PROPRIETOR(s): Debbie James of 98 Farnol Road, Shard Oak, Brilindon, BR3 1XD.
2.  (27th August 202#) The price stated to have been paid on 14th August 202# was £295,000.
3.  (15th May 1999) The Transfer to the proprietor contains a covenant to observe and perform the covenants referred to in the Charges Register and of an indemnity in respect thereof.

---

## C:  Charges Register
**This register contains any charges and other matters that affect the land.**

1.  (13th October 1953) By a Conveyance dated 20th September 1953 made between Fressie Taylor (1) and Richard Bert (2) contains restrictive covenants.

**NO COPY FILED UPON FIRST REGISTRATION**

2.  (1st December 1989) By a Transfer dated 16th November 1989 made between Ethel George (1) and Arjun Mehta (2) contains the following covenants:
      'Not to use the property as anything other than as a private dwellinghouse for one family only.
      Not without the written consent of the Transferor or its agent to allow any hut, bungalow, shed, caravan house on wheels or anything intended for use as a dwellinghouse or sleeping apartment to be erected on the land.
      Not to keep poultry or livestock on the property or surrounding land.'
3.  (27th August 202#) REGISTERED CHARGE dated 14th August 202# to secure the moneys including the further advances therein mentioned.
4.  (27th August 202#) Proprietor(s): Hanbury Building Society of Unit 4b, Kingfisher Business Park, Birmingham, B8 5TF.

**END OF REGISTER**

**Attachment 2**

Karia Law LLP
39 Layton Avenue
Shard Oak
Brilindon
BR3 8YC

Dawson Lloyd Solicitors
8 Portland Road
Aston Rock
Brilindon
BR7 9KS

10 November 202#

Dear Sirs,

**Purchase of 98 Farnol Road ('the Property'), Subject to Contract**

Thank you for your letter dated 1 November. We have taken our client's instructions and reply in accordance with your numbered points as follows:

1.  Please see enclosed the title plan as requested.
2.  We note your comments in relation to the missing documentation. However, our client is not willing to obtain an indemnity insurance policy due to the length of time that has passed since the conveyance. If your client requires an indemnity insurance policy, this will need to be obtained by themselves, at their own expense.
3.  Our client confirms that they are not aware of any breaches of the covenants referred to in the charges register.
4.  We confirm that we undertake to discharge the charge dated 14 August 202# in favour of Hanbury Building Society upon receipt of the completion monies.

Finally, our clients have advised their preferred date for completion as 17th April. Please take your client's instructions as to their availability.
We look forward to hearing from you in due course.

Yours faithfully

Karia Law LLP

\*   \*   \*

# ▇ YOUR TURN

Have a go at answering question 2, remembering the guidance on pages 55–56.
- Refer to the structured approach in the SRA's assessment criteria on page 56.
- Create a list of the most important pieces of information to assist with writing the report to your client.
- Timings are important: you will need to prepare and write your answer in 30 minutes.

| SQE1 Functioning legal knowledge link |
| --- |
| Remember from chapters 2 and 4 of **Revise SQE: Property Practice** that restrictive covenants usually run with the land and are therefore binding on future owners. Clients need to be made aware of these covenants as they may impact on their enjoyment of the land. |

## EVALUATING YOUR ANSWER

When you have attempted question 2, mark it yourself against the SQE2 legal writing assessment criteria. Do you think your attempt met the threshold standard?

Now compare your attempt with the following key legal points and two sample answers to question 2. A circled number indicates that commentary is provided for this part of the answer. The commentary will explain whether the sample is likely to meet the threshold SQE2 standard.

> ➡**Key legal points: Question 2**
>
> - It is important to remember the audience of the letter. In this case, as the letter is being sent to a client to provide a report on title, it is important to use clear language and avoid legalese, to assist their understanding.
> - Missing documents on the Land Registry legal title can have financial implications such as for breach of covenant. If there are restrictive covenants preventing an owner from being able to do something to the land, without sight of the document it is not possible to know what these covenants are and whether someone is in breach. In instances such as this, it is recommended that an indemnity insurance policy be taken out. Obtaining indemnity insurance will protect current and future owners from experiencing financial loss, should someone come along with a copy of the document containing restrictive covenants and bring action against the owner for breach of covenants that they were unaware of.
> - Although sellers should be asked to take out the indemnity insurance at their own expense, in instances where they refuse, clients should be advised to take out an indemnity insurance policy at their own expense to protect themselves. It is also a likely requirement when a lender is involved.
> - In instances where there are restrictive covenants on the title that are problematic for the client, there are a few options available. The client can decide to withdraw from the purchase providing exchange of contracts has not yet taken place. They can identify who has the benefit of the covenant and ask if they would be willing to vary the covenant (with older covenants this can be difficult). Another option, although somewhat expensive, is making an application to the Upper Tribunal (Lands Chamber) for this to be modified. Finally, an indemnity policy could be sought from the sellers in the event of this covenant being breached in the future.

## ■ SAMPLE ANSWER 1 TO QUESTION 2

Dawson Lloyd Solicitors
8 Portland Road
Aston Rock
Brilindon
BR7 9KS

Mr & Mrs M Conway
55a Benedict Way
Castle Green
Brilindon
BR2 2EG

15 November 202#

Dear Mr and Mrs Conway,

**Re: Purchase of 98 Farnol Road**

I refer to your purchase of the above property and I am reporting to you with the following:

1.  Official Copy of Register – Title Number W4669433. The extent of the property you are purchasing is shown edged red on the plan. The property is sold subject to and with the benefit of the Transfer dated 16 November 1989 which contains restrictions affecting the property as follows:
    • You can only use the property as a private home, for the use of one family. This means that you will not be able to use the property for business purposes.
    • You will need written consent of the original transferor (original owners) to build a hut, bungalow or shed intended for use as a dwellinghouse on the property.
    • You cannot keep chickens or any livestock on the property. ❶

    I note your intention to construct a bungalow at the bottom of the garden. However, under the restrictive covenants in the 1989 transfer, this will not be permitted.

    There are a few options available to you:
    a. Withdraw from the purchase BEFORE exchange of contracts takes place.
    b. Identify who has the benefit of the covenant and ask if they would be willing to vary the covenant (however, as the covenant was created a while ago, this could be difficult).
    c. Make an application to the Upper Tribunal (Lands Chamber) for this to be modified. However, this may be expensive.
    d. Take out an indemnity policy in the event of this covenant being breached in the future. This would most likely be the quickest option if you wish to proceed with the purchase. ❷

2.  The Official Copy Entries also refer to a Conveyance dated 20 September 1953 which contains restrictions affecting the property. However, copies of this document were not filed with the Land Registry when they were first created and therefore these restrictions are 'unknown'. These may well adversely affect the property, and the only way to protect your position and that of the Bank is to take out indemnity insurance. Usually, this would be taken out at the seller's expense. However, they have refused this due to the length of time that has passed since the conveyance. It

is therefore our advice that you take out an indemnity insurance policy, so that you are protected if any of these restrictions come to light in the future and are enforced. The indemnity policy will reimburse any financial loss suffered in relation to this. It will also likely be a requirement of your lender. Please confirm your agreement to this and we can arrange it for you. ❸

3. I have asked the seller's solicitor to confirm that the restrictions in the 1989 Transfer have been complied with, and they have confirmed that the sellers are not aware of any issues. ❹

4. The Title to the property is clear and marketable.

5. Please let me know, as soon as possible, if there are any further points/queries you wish me to raise with the seller's solicitor. Once contracts are exchanged there is no obligation on the seller to reply to any further enquiries. ❺

6. Finally, the sellers have advised their preferred date for completion to be 17 April. Please advise whether this date is suitable for you both.

In summary, please confirm the following:

    i. Your decision in relation to the restrictive covenant preventing the building of a bungalow.

    ii. Any further points/queries you wish me to raise with the sellers' solicitor.

    iii. Your agreement to taking out an indemnity insurance policy in relation to the missing 1953 Conveyance.

    iv. Whether you are happy with a completion date of 17 April. ❻

I look forward to hearing from you with any queries which you may have.

Yours sincerely

Trainee Solicitor

## COMMENTARY

❶ The first paragraph sets out the reason for the letter and provides a breakdown of the restrictions that the clients will need to adhere to, using clear and concise language. This is essential when providing information to clients, in line with the assessment objectives for legal writing.

❷ This section explicitly refers to the client's intentions in relation to building a bungalow. It clearly identifies that this is not permitted under the restrictive covenants and goes on to provide advice on different client options. It sets out these options in a legally correct and comprehensive way as per the legal writing assessment objectives, and provides the examiner with clear evidence that this has been achieved.

❸ It is extremely important that clients are made aware of any issues with the title in a clear and precise manner. Here there is a missing conveyance that has restrictive covenants in it. Without knowing what they are, it is impossible to advise clients on what these could be. This could lead to a client inadvertently breaching a covenant, and could become costly. Indemnity insurance policies should be taken out in these instances, to protect a client (and lender) from any financial repercussions because of the breach. The candidate has explained this to the client clearly, using appropriate language, showing the examiner that they can apply appropriate advice to the client's situation. The candidate also raises the point that when acting for lenders, if a client refuses an indemnity insurance policy, this will need to be reported to the lender for approval to continue and could potentially become a professional conduct issue if this is not done. By including this, the candidate shows an ability to identify and resolve professional conduct issues in line with the assessment objectives.

④ This paragraph concisely explains the situation to the client and reassures them that there are no past breaches of any covenants to be concerned about. It logically follows on from the explanation of the covenants that exist and uses appropriate language to assist the client's understanding.

⑤ This paragraph clearly emphasises that once exchange of contracts takes place, there may not be an opportunity to make further enquiries. This shows the examiner that the candidate understands the procedure by applying the law correctly to the client's situation, which is another of the assessment objectives.

⑥ The end of this letter summarises the points that the client needs to respond to in a clear and direct manner. By setting it out in this way, the candidate has made it easy for the client to identify what they need to do to progress matters.

## Does this answer meet the threshold?

The sample answer above includes all the components that the report on title should cover. It appropriately explains legal terms in a clear way and provides the client with the required information to allow them to make an informed decision. It provides practical solutions in relation to the restrictive covenants and appropriately identifies that an indemnity policy may be the most practical solution. It is therefore likely to meet the threshold standard for the SQE2 legal writing assessment.

Note how each of the assessment criteria for legal writing are dealt with and, where appropriate, where the examiner is directed specifically to the areas of the letter which deal with those criteria. It is important to remember the criteria by which you are being assessed and to evidence your competency in this to the examiner.

Now consider the second sample answer to question 2.

## ■ SAMPLE ANSWER 2 TO QUESTION 2

Dawson Lloyd Solicitors
8 Portland Road
Aston Rock
Brilindon
BR7 9KS

Mr & Mrs M Conway
55a Benedict Way,
Castle Green,
Birmingham,
BR2 2EG

15 November 202#

Dear Mark & Sue, ❶

**Re: Purchase of 98 Farnol Road**

I refer to your purchase of the above property and I am reporting to you with the following:

Official Copy of Register – Title Number W4669433. The extent of the property you are purchasing is shown edged red on the plan. The property is sold subject to and with the benefit of the Transfer dated 16 November 1989 which contains covenants affecting the property. Please see the charges register to identify what these are. ❷

You will see that you are not going to be able to build a bungalow on the property because there is a restrictive covenant on the property that forbids this. Please do let me know if you are happy to proceed on the basis of buying the property and promising not to build a bungalow. If you breach the restrictive covenant, you may have proceedings brought against you to force you to remove it, which would leave your mother effectively homeless. ❸

The Official Copy Entries also refer to a conveyance dated 20 September 1953 which contains covenants and restrictions which affect the property. However, copies of this document were not filed with the Land Registry upon first registration and therefore these restrictions are 'unknown'. This may well affect the value of the property and an indemnity insurance policy should be taken out at the seller's expense. However, they are being awkward and refusing to take out a policy on the basis that the conveyance is over 50 years old. You could take out an indemnity policy of your own. But, based on what the seller's solicitors have said, I think it highly unlikely that someone will now come along to enforce the covenant. I would recommend that you just ignore this, as if you decide to tell the bank, they will probably force you to take out an indemnity policy which will just be an unnecessary expense based on the above. Please do let me know if you would rather take out an indemnity policy at your own expense. ❹

The covenants in the 1989 Transfer have been adhered to and the sellers will not provide any further information in relation to this. It is prudent for you to make your own investigations into the title and contact neighbours of properties in the vicinity to see if they are aware of any previous breaches. ❺

Please let me know, as soon as possible, if you plan to go ahead with the purchase irrespective of the restrictions that you will be placed under. I must inform you that if you pull out of the purchase before you exchange contracts, you will not be forced to buy the property. But we will still require payment either way. ❻

Finally, the sellers have advised their preferred date for completion to be 17th April. Are you happy with this? ❼

Yours faithfully, ❽

Trainee Solicitor

## COMMENTARY

❶ The beginning of this letter is too informal. It would be more appropriate to address the clients as Mr and Mrs Conway.

❷ This paragraph is not client-friendly. It is not easy for the client to understand, and uses inappropriate legalese when asking them to look at an additional document. It is unclear as to what covenants are and this could be quite confusing for a lay client to interpret. It is unlikely that this paragraph would satisfy the SQE legal writing assessment criteria as it does not use clear language appropriate for the client.

❸ The letter correctly identifies that the client will be in breach of a restrictive covenant if they go ahead with building the bungalow. However, it fails to provide the clients with legal advice and the different options available to them. Also, the wording is emotive and could cause the client distress, thinking about the mother's potential homelessness. Because of these aspects, this paragraph does not meet the assessment criteria.

④ This paragraph is problematic as it provides incorrect advice that could potentially lead to a professional negligence claim. This does not meet the assessment criteria as it does not provide the correct law, and clients could interpret this advice as not needing indemnity insurance. If, at any point in the future, the conveyance was discovered and someone claimed the clients were in breach of the covenants, the clients would be forced to remedy this situation at their own expense. This section also makes no mention of the requirement to inform the lender. This could potentially result in a professional conduct issue, as a solicitor has a duty to both the client and the lender to act in their best interests. The lender might not want to proceed with the mortgage offer unless an indemnity insurance policy is taken out. Ultimately, it is the client's and lender's choice. However, the candidate should make it clear that they advise taking out an indemnity policy, and fully explain the risks if this does not happen.

⑤ This paragraph does not explain the law correctly. While a conveyancing transaction follows the principle *'Caveat emptor* / Buyer beware', it is not the client's responsibility to go 'door to door' to speak to neighbours. It is enough that the sellers have confirmed that there have been no breaches to their knowledge. If at any point it transpired that they were aware and had actively misled the clients, they could be held liable in misrepresentation as they have misled replies to enquiries. This paragraph lacks clear guidance as to repercussions, and puts the onus on the client to do something that they will be unfamiliar with which is not necessary.

⑥ While not entirely incorrect, this paragraph is poorly written. It is correct in so far as clients can withdraw from a sale or purchase up until the point of exchange of contracts. However, solicitors will usually not require full payment of their fees when the transaction has not proceeded to completion. It is usual practice to charge a proportion of the fees to reflect the work done to date. There is a risk with this paragraph that the clients will feel forced to proceed with completion because they think they will have to pay the fees regardless.

⑦ This does not showcase acting in the client's best interests. It does not provide an explanation that the clients have any other choice but to agree with the seller's preferred date for completion. This section is also informally written; it would be more appropriate to use professional language to take the client's instructions as to their preferred completion date.

⑧ Incorrect salutation used. When writing to individual clients, 'Yours sincerely' should be used. Also, the letter does not summarise clearly what the client needs to respond to.

## Does this answer meet the threshold?

When assessing the second report on title against the SQE2 legal writing assessment criteria, it is unlikely that this letter would meet the threshold standard for the SQE2 legal writing assessment. There would be a potential claim made against the firm for negligence if the client was to follow the advice, not take out an indemnity policy and then have a claim brought against them for breach of covenant.

## ■ KEY POINT CHECKLIST

This chapter has covered the following key knowledge points:
• The SQE2 assessment criteria for legal writing and how to apply them in the context of property practice.
• A suggested structure for approaching an SQE2 legal writing assessment question.
• Sample answers which show what kind of requisitions on title and reports on title are either likely or unlikely to meet the threshold standard, with full commentary on their strengths and weaknesses.

# ■ SUMMARY AND REFLECTION

The key to success in the SQE2 legal writing assessment in the context of property is to make sure that you read all of the information, then cross-reference any necessary documents before beginning to write your answer. It is also worth making a brief plan to include all of the legal points that you want to raise. This will ensure that you do not miss any of the points once you have begun writing your answer.

It is important to remember the assessment criteria here. You need to show that you are able to apply the law to the relevant property question, in addition to being able to write in a professional manner. You will need to ensure that any advice provided to a client is clear and concise, and shows the examiner why it is applicable to the scenario.

Make sure you practise writing letters to the appropriate audience. When writing to clients, you need to be clear and avoid overuse of legal jargon. When writing to the other side's solicitors, legal jargon and legalistic terms will be expected. You need to be able to adapt your writing style accordingly: if your letter is not audience-appropriate, you will be penalised for this in the assessment.

It is worth reviewing the commentaries in this chapter and noting down any legal points that you have missed. You could reflect on these further and where necessary, review the content in the relevant *Revise SQE: Property Practice* or *Revise SQE: Land Law* chapters to ensure your understanding.

# 4

# Legal drafting

## ■ MAKE SURE YOU KNOW

This chapter deals with the skill of legal drafting in the context of property law. Legal drafting in property law is one of the legal skills that may be assessed on day two of the SQE2 assessments (see the Introduction for more detail). The SQE2 can test candidates' knowledge of both the processes associated with property law and the application of land law principles to these processes. We recommend that you read this revision guide once you have familiarised yourself with the contents of **Revise SQE: Land Law** and **Revise SQE: Property Practice**. You will also see that drafting contracts and transfers contained in those texts are developed further within this book, to show you how SQE2 skills assessments incorporate the legal principles you will have learned for your SQE1 examinations.

This chapter provides examples of how to draft a contract and also how to draft the legal document to transfer the legal title on completion to the new owner(s). It identifies rules relating to legally binding contracts and the transfer of title, which could arise in the context of an SQE2 legal drafting assessment.

## ■ SQE ASSESSMENT ADVICE

As you work through this chapter, pay attention in your revision to:
- the documents provided to assist you in the drafting of the contract or transfer
- the way in which the contracts or transfers are tailored depending on the circumstances
- addressing all relevant legal and factual issues
- complying with appropriate formalities, in particular in relation to the execution panel of a transfer
- using clear, accurate and succinct language
- ensuring the law is applied correctly to the client's situation
- the way in which any ethical or professional conduct issues are identified and resolved.

See the Appendix for the SRA's performance indicators in legal drafting.

## ■ INTRODUCTION TO LEGAL DRAFTING IN PROPERTY PRACTICE

The SQE2 assessments for this topic aim to replicate scenarios from practice, reflecting day-to-day aspects in the field of property. As with all areas of law, a key aspect of practising in this area is the ability to draft legal documents. Your SQE2 legal drafting assessment will be to draft a legal document or parts of a legal document. This may take the form of drafting from a precedent or amending a document already drafted. However, it may also involve drafting without either of these. While the question itself will give you some direction about what you need to cover in this task, you will be required to apply your knowledge to the scenario and adequately draft a valid contract or transfer deed to transfer the legal ownership to new owners. This chapter will provide examples of how you can do this and meet the assessment criteria for the SQE2 legal drafting assessment.

Your answer to the SQE2 legal drafting assessment will be more successful if you take time to adopt the following approach:

1. Once you have read the question, write down the key points that will need to be incorporated in the contract or transfer.
2. You can then form the structure of the contract or transfer to ensure all of the key points are included.
3. Write your answer.
4. Review your answer, keeping in mind the SQE2 legal drafting assessment criteria.

## Assessment technique

When drafting a contract or transfer, ensure that you are utilising all documents available to you (for example, with a transfer, both the contract and office copy entries will assist to ensure that the transfer is consistent with the office copy entries). This demonstrates good practice to the examiner, as it would prevent the Land Registry from raising unnecessary requisitions that could cause a delay to registering the client's ownership and the lender's charge.

## SQE2 legal drafting assessment criteria

Ensure that you follow these criteria when drafting your answer:

### Skills

1. Use clear, precise, concise and acceptable language.
2. Structure the document appropriately and logically.

### Application of law

3. Draft a document which is legally correct.
4. Draft a document which is legally comprehensive, identifying any ethical and professional conduct issues and exercising judgement to resolve them honestly and with integrity.

In chapters 4 and 5 of *Revise SQE: Property Practice*, we considered the different sections of both contracts and form TR1, and the key points to include. Question 1 below demonstrates how your knowledge of this topic could be tested in the context and format of an SQE2 legal drafting assessment. You might wish to view pages 2 and 3 of the Standard Conditions of Sale form in Attachment 2 (listing the conditions) in digital format at www.lawsociety.org.uk/topics/property/standard-conditions-of-sale, for easier legibility.

# ■ QUESTION 1

## Email to candidate

**From:** Partner
**Sent:** 24 September 202#
**To:** Candidate
**Subject:** Sale of Franhurst Farm

I am acting on behalf of Mr Matthew Worthington in the sale of his property to Mr Josef Christou and Mrs Doulla Christou of 44 Barry Street, Prestford, M25 0BA.

The client is selling the property for £305,000 and has agreed with the buyers to include a cream leather sofa for an additional £1,500. I should also mention that Mr Worthington lives in the property with his daughter Daniella Worthington (aged 23).

The client has advised that he wishes to complete the transaction on the 29th October 202#.

**I would be grateful if you could review the enclosed office copy entries (Attachment 1) with a view to drafting the contract (Attachment 2) to send to the buyers' solicitors, Star Legal.**

Thanks

Partner

### Attachment 1

Contains public sector information licensed under the Open Government Licence v3.0.

| Official copy of register of title | Title number L894332 | Edition date 21.03.1977 |
|---|---|---|

- This official copy shows the entries in the register of title on 13.2.202# at 22:01:16.
- This date must be quoted as the "search from date" in any official search application based on this copy.
- The date at the beginning of an entry is the date on which the entry was made in the register.
- Issued on (13th February 202#).
- Under s.67 of the Land Registration Act 2002, this copy is admissible in evidence to the same extent as the original.
- For more information about the register of title see Land Registry website www.landregistry .gov.uk or Land Registry Guide 1 – *A guide to the information we keep and how you can obtain it.*
- This title is dealt with by the Land Registry Fylde Office.

## A:  Property Register
**This register describes the land and estate comprised in the Title.**

Westshire    :    Brumlington

1.  (13th February 202#) The freehold land shown edged with red on the plan of the above title filed at the registry and known as Franhurst Farm, Hurst Lane, Brumlington, Westshire, BL0 9HJ.

---

## B:  Proprietorship Register
**This register specifies the class of title and identifies the owner. It contains any entries that affect the right of disposal.**

**Title Absolute**
1.  (13th February 202#) PROPRIETOR(s): Matthew Worthington of Franhurst Farm, Hurst Lane, Brumlington, Westshire, BL0 9HJ.
2.  (13th February 202#) The price stated to have been paid on 2nd February 202# was £200,000.
3.  (3rd October 1997) The Transfer to the proprietor contains a covenant to observe and perform the covenants referred to in the Charges Register and of an indemnity in respect thereof.

---

## C:  Charges Register
**This register contains any charges and other matters that affect the land**

1.  (8th December 1956) A conveyance of the land in this title and other land dated 29th November 1956 made between (1) Greville Lane (Vendor) and (2) Maurice Williams (Purchaser) contains the following covenant:

    No hotel tavern public house or beer house for the sale of wines, spirits ales or stout or any malt or excisable liquor of any kind be built nor shall any such trade be carried on upon the Property of a noisome or offensive nature nor shall any house building or plot be used for any purpose that may be a nuisance to the Vendors or their successors in title or the neighbouring owners or tenants.

2.  (3rd October 1997) By a Transfer dated 24th September 1997 made between Wayne Hogarth (1) and Arabella Davies (2) contains the following covenants:

    A covenant not to keep animals other than usual domestic pets on the property.

**END OF REGISTER**

**Attachment 2**

# CONTRACT

**Incorporating the Standard Conditions of Sale (Fifth Edition – 2018 revision)**
© **The Law Society**

┌──────── **For Conveyancer's use only** ────────┐

Buyer's conveyancer: _____

Seller's conveyancer: _____

Law Society Formula [A/B/C / Personal Exchange]
This information does not form part of the
Contract

└──────────────────────────────────────────────┘

| | |
|---|---|
| **Date** | : |
| **Seller** | : |
| **Buyer** | : |
| **Property (freehold/leasehold)** | : |
| **Title number/root of title** | : |
| **Specified incumbrances** | : |
| **Title guarantee (full/limited)** | : |
| **Completion date** | : |
| **Contract rate** | : |
| **Purchase price** | : |
| **Deposit** | : |
| **Contents price (if separate)** | : |
| **Balance** | : |

The seller will sell and the buyer will buy the property for the purchase price.

| WARNING | Signed |
|---|---|
| This is a formal document, designed to create legal rights and legal obligations. Take advice before using it. | |
| | Seller/Buyer |

# STANDARD CONDITIONS OF SALE (FIFTH EDITION - 2018 REVISION)
## (NATIONAL CONDITIONS OF SALE 25TH EDITION, LAW SOCIETY'S CONDITIONS OF SALE 2011)

**GENERAL**

**1 Definitions**

1.1 In these conditions:
- (a) 'accrued interest' means:
  - (i) if money has been placed on deposit or in a building society share account, the interest actually earned
  - (ii) otherwise, the interest which might reasonably have been earned by depositing the money at interest on seven days' notice of withdrawal with a clearing bank less, in either case, any proper charges for handling the money
- (b) 'clearing bank' means a bank admitted by the Bank of England as a direct participant in its CHAPS system
- (c) 'completion date' has the meaning given in condition 6.1.1
- (d) 'contents price' means any separate amount payable for contents included in the contract
- (e) 'contract rate' means the Law Society's interest rate from time to time in force
- (f) 'conveyancer' means a solicitor, barrister, duly certified notary public, licensed conveyancer or recognised body under sections 9 or 23 of the Administration of Justice Act 1985
- (g) 'lease' includes sub-lease, tenancy and agreement for a lease or sub-lease
- (h) 'mortgage' means a mortgage or charge securing the repayment of money
- (i) 'notice to complete' means a notice requiring completion of the contract in accordance with condition 6.8
- (j) 'public requirement' means any notice, order or proposal given or made (whether before or after the date of the contract) by a body acting on statutory authority
- (k) 'requisition' includes objection
- (l) 'transfer' includes conveyance and assignment
- (m) 'working day' means any day from Monday to Friday (inclusive) which is not Christmas Day, Good Friday or a statutory Bank Holiday.

1.2 In these conditions the terms 'absolute title' and 'official copies' have the special meanings given to them by the Land Registration Act 2002.

1.3 A party is ready, able and willing to complete:
- (a) if he could be, but for the default of the other party, and
- (b) in the case of the seller, even though the property remains subject to a mortgage, if the amount to be paid on completion enables the property to be transferred freed of all mortgages (except any to which the sale is expressly subject).

1.4 These conditions apply except as varied or excluded by the contract.

**2 Joint parties**

If there is more than one seller or more than one buyer, the obligations which they undertake can be enforced against them all jointly or against each individually.

**3 Notices and documents**

3.1 A notice required or authorised by the contract must be in writing.

3.2 Giving a notice or delivering a document to a party's conveyancer has the same effect as giving or delivering it to that party.

3.3 Where delivery of the original document is not essential, a notice or document is validly given or sent if it is sent:
- (a) by fax, or
- (b) by e-mail to an e-mail address for the intended recipient given in the contract

3.4 Subject to conditions 1.3.5 to 1.3.7, a notice is given and a document is delivered when it is received.

3.5 (a) A notice or document sent through a document exchange is received when it is available for collection.
- (b) A notice or document which is received after 4.00pm on a working day, or on a day which is not a working day, is to be treated as having been received on the next working day.
- (c) An automated response to a notice or document sent by e-mail that the intended recipient is out of the office is to be treated as proof that the notice or document was not received.

3.6 Condition 1.3.7 applies unless there is proof:
- (a) that a notice or document has not been received, or
- (b) of when it was received.

3.7 A notice or document sent by the following means is treated as having been received as follows:

| | | |
|---|---|---|
| (a) by first-class post: | before 4.00pm on the second working day after posting |
| (b) by second-class post: | before 4.00pm on the third working day after posting |
| (c) through a document exchange: | before 4.00pm on the first working day after the day on which it would normally be available for collection by the addressee |
| (d) by fax: | one hour after despatch |
| (e) by e-mail: | before 4.00pm on the first working day after despatch. |

**4 VAT**

4.1 The purchase price and the contents price are inclusive of any value added tax.

4.2 All other sums made payable by the contract are exclusive of any value added tax and where a supply is made which is chargeable to value added tax, the recipient of the supply is to pay the supplier (in addition to any other amounts payable under the contract) a sum equal to the value added tax chargeable on that supply.

**5 Assignment and sub-sales**

5.1 The buyer is not entitled to transfer the benefit of the contract

5.2 The seller cannot be required to transfer the property in parts or to any person other than the buyer.

**6 Third party rights**

Unless otherwise expressly stated nothing in this contract will create rights pursuant to the Contracts (Rights of Third Parties) Act 1999 in favour of anyone other than the parties to the contract.

**2. FORMATION**

**2.1 Date**

2.1.1 If the parties intend to make a contract by exchanging duplicate copies by post or through a document exchange, the contract is made when the last copy is posted or deposited at the document exchange.

2.1.2 If the parties' conveyancers agree to treat exchange as taking place before duplicate copies are actually exchanged, the contract is made as so agreed.

**2.2 Deposit**

2.2.1 The buyer is to pay or send a deposit of 10 per cent of the purchase price no later than the date of the contract.

2.2.2 If a cheque tendered in payment of all or part of the deposit is dishonoured when first presented, the seller may, within seven working days of being notified that the cheque has been dishonoured, give notice to the buyer that the contract is discharged by the buyer's breach.

2.2.3 Conditions 2.2.4 to 2.2.6 do not apply on a sale by auction.

2.2.4 The deposit is to be paid:
- (a) by electronic means from an account held in the name of a conveyancer at a clearing bank to an account in the name of the seller's conveyancer or (in a case where condition 2.2.5 applies) a conveyancer nominated by him and maintained at a clearing bank or
- (b) to the seller's conveyancer or (in a case where condition 2.2.5 applies) a conveyancer nominated by him by cheque drawn on a solicitor's or licensed conveyancer's client account

2.2.5 If before completion date the seller agrees to buy another property in England and Wales for his residence, he may use all or any part of the deposit as a deposit in that transaction to be held on terms to the same effect as this condition and condition 2.2.6.

2.2.6 Any deposit or part of a deposit not being used in accordance with condition 2.2.5 is to be held by the seller's conveyancer as stakeholder on terms that on completion it is paid to the seller with accrued interest.

**2.3 Auctions**

2.3.1 On a sale by auction the following conditions apply to the property and, if it is sold in lots, to each lot.

2.3.2 The sale is subject to a reserve price.

2.3.3 The seller, or a person on his behalf, may bid up to the reserve price.

2.3.5 If there is a dispute about a bid, the auctioneer may resolve the dispute or restart the auction at the last undisputed bid.

2.3.6 The deposit is to be paid to the auctioneer as agent for the seller.

**3. MATTERS AFFECTING THE PROPERTY**

**3.1 Freedom from incumbrances**

3.1.1 The seller is selling the property free from incumbrances, other than those mentioned in condition 3.1.2.

3.1.2 The incumbrances subject to which the property is sold are:
- (a) those specified in the contract
- (b) those discoverable by inspection of the property before the date of the contract.
- (c) those the seller does not and could not reasonably know about
- (d) those, other than mortgages, which the buyer knows about
- (e) entries made before the date of the contract in any public register except those maintained by the Land Registry or its Land Charges Department or by Companies House
- (f) public requirements.

3.1.3 After the contract is made, the seller is to give the buyer written details without delay of any new public requirement and of anything in writing which he learns about concerning a matter covered by condition 3.1.2.

3.1.4 The buyer is to bear the cost of complying with any outstanding public requirement and is to indemnify the seller against any liability resulting from a public requirement.

**3.2 Physical state**

3.2.1 The buyer accepts the property in the physical state it is in at the date of the contract unless the seller is building or converting it.

3.2.2 A leasehold property is sold subject to any subsisting breach of a condition or tenant's obligation relating to the physical state of the property which renders the lease liable to forfeiture.

3.2.3 A sub-lease is granted subject to any subsisting breach of a condition or tenant's obligation relating to the physical state of the property which renders the seller's own lease liable to forfeiture.

**3.3 Leases affecting the property**

3.3.1 The following provisions apply if any part of the property is sold subject to a lease.

3.3.2 (a) The seller having provided the buyer with full details of each lease or copies of the documents embodying the lease terms, the buyer is treated as entering into the contract knowing and fully accepting those terms.
- (b) The seller is to inform the buyer without delay if the lease ends or if the seller learns of any application by the tenant in connection with the lease; the seller is then to act as the buyer reasonably directs, and the buyer is to indemnify him against all consequent loss and expense.
- (c) Except with the buyer's consent, the seller is not to agree to any proposal to change the lease terms nor to take any step to end the lease.
- (d) The seller is to inform the buyer without delay of any change to the lease terms which may be proposed or agreed.
- (e) The buyer is to indemnify the seller against all claims arising from the lease after actual completion; this includes claims which are unenforceable against a buyer for want of registration.
- (f) The seller takes no responsibility for what rent is lawfully recoverable, nor for whether or how any legislation affects the lease.
- (g) If the let land is not wholly within the property, the seller may apportion the rent.

**4. TITLE AND TRANSFER**

**4.1 Proof of title**

4.1.1 Without cost to the buyer, the seller is to provide the buyer with proof of the title to the property and of his ability to transfer it, or to procure its transfer.

4.1.2 Where the property has a registered title the proof is to include official copies of the items referred to in rules 134(1)(a) and (b) and 135(1)(a) of the Land Registration Rules 2003, so far as they are not to be discharged or overridden at or before completion.

4.1.3 Where the property has an unregistered title, the proof is to include:
- (a) an abstract of title or an epitome of title with photocopies of the documents, and
- (b) production of every document or an abstract, epitome or copy of it with an original marking by a conveyancer either against the original or an examined abstract or an examined copy.

**4.2 Requisitions**

4.2.1 The buyer may not raise requisitions:
- (a) on any title shown by the seller before the contract was made
- (b) in relation to the matters covered by condition 3.1.2.

4.2.2 Notwithstanding condition 4.2.1, the buyer may, within six working days of a matter coming to his attention after the contract was made, raise written requisitions on that matter. In that event, steps 3 and 4 in condition 4.3.1 apply.

4.2.3 On the expiry of the relevant time limit under condition 4.2.2 or condition 4.3.1, the buyer loses his right to raise requisitions or to make observations.

**4.3 Timetable**

4.3.1 Subject to condition 4.2 and to the extent that the seller did not take the steps described in condition 4.1.1 before the contract was made, the following are the steps for deducing and investigating the title to the property to be taken within the following time limits:

| Step | | Time Limit |
|---|---|---|
| 1. | The seller is to comply with condition 4.1.1 | Immediately after making the contract |
| 2. | The buyer may raise written requisitions | Six working days after either the date of the contract or the date of delivery of the seller's evidence of title on which the requisitions are raised, whichever is the later |
| 3. | The seller is to reply in writing to any requisitions raised | Four working days after receiving the requisitions |
| 4. | The buyer may make written observations on the seller's replies | Three working days after receiving the replies |

The time limit on the buyer's right to raise requisitions applies even where the seller supplies incomplete evidence of his title, but the buyer may, within six working days from delivery of any further evidence, raise further requisitions resulting from that evidence.

4.3.2 The parties are to take the following steps to prepare and agree the transfer of the property within the following time limits:

| Step | | Time Limit |
|---|---|---|
| A. | The buyer is to send the seller a draft transfer | At least twelve working days before completion date |
| B. | The seller is to approve or revise that draft and either return it or retain it for use as the actual transfer | Four working days after delivery of the draft transfer |
| C. | If the draft is returned the buyer is to send an engrossment to the seller | At least five working days before completion date |

4.3.3 Periods of time under conditions 4.3.1 and 4.3.2 may run concurrently.

4.3.4 If the period between the date of the contract and completion date is less than 15 working days, the time limits in conditions 4.2.2, 4.3.1 and 4.3.2 are to be reduced by the same proportion as that period bears to the period of 15 working days. Fractions of a working day are to be rounded down except that the time limit to perform any step is not to be less than one working day.

**4.4 Defining the property**

The seller need not:
- (a) prove the exact boundaries of the property
- (b) prove who owns fences, ditches, hedges or walls
- (c) separately identify parts of the property with different titles further than he may be able to do from information in his possession.

**4.5 Rents and rentcharges**

The fact that a rent or rentcharge, whether payable or receivable by the owner of the property, has been, or will on completion be, informally apportioned is not to be regarded as a defect in title.

**4.6 Transfer**

4.6.1 The buyer does not prejudice his right to raise requisitions, or to require replies to any raised, by taking any steps in relation to preparing or agreeing the transfer.

4.6.2 Subject to condition 4.6.3, the seller is to transfer the property with full title guarantee.

4.6.3 The transfer is to have effect as if the disposition is expressly made subject to all matters covered by condition 3.1.2 and, if the property is leasehold, is to contain a statement that the covenants set out in section 4 of the Law of Property (Miscellaneous Provisions) Act 1994 will not extend to any breach of the tenant's covenants in the lease relating to the physical state of the property.

4.6.4 If after completion the seller will remain bound by any obligation affecting the property which was disclosed to the buyer before the contract was made, but the law does not imply any covenant by the buyer to indemnify the seller against liability for future breaches of it:

(a) the buyer is to covenant in the transfer to indemnify the seller against liability for any future breach of the obligation and to perform it from then on, and

(b) if required by the seller, the buyer is to execute and deliver to the seller on completion a duplicate transfer prepared by the buyer.

4.6.5 The seller is to arrange at his expense that, in relation to every document of title which the buyer does not receive on completion, the buyer is to have the benefit of:

(a) a written acknowledgement of his right to its production, and

(b) a written undertaking for its safe custody (except while it is held by a mortgagee or by someone in a fiduciary capacity).

4.7 **Membership of company**

Where the seller is, or is required to be, a member of a company that has an interest in the property or has management responsibilities for the property or the surrounding areas, the seller is, without cost to the buyer, to provide such documents on completion as will enable the buyer to become a member of that company.

**5. RISK, INSURANCE AND OCCUPATION PENDING COMPLETION**

5.1.1 The property is at the risk of the buyer from the date of the contract

5.1.2 The seller is under no obligation to the buyer to insure the property unless:

(a) the contract provides that a policy effected by or for the seller and insuring the property or any part of it against liability for loss or damage is to continue in force, or

(b) the property or any part of it is let on terms under which the seller (whether as landlord or as tenant) is obliged to insure against loss or damage.

5.1.3 If the seller is obliged to insure the property under condition 5.1.2, the seller is to:

(a) do everything necessary to maintain the policy

(b) permit the buyer to inspect the policy or evidence of its terms

(c) if before completion the property suffers loss or damage:

(i) pay to the buyer on completion the amount of the policy monies which the seller has received, so far as not applied in repairing or reinstating the property, and

(ii) if no final payment has then been received, assign to the buyer, at the buyer's expense, all rights to claim under the policy in such form as the buyer reasonably requires and pending execution of the assignment hold any policy monies received in trust for the buyer

(d) cancel the policy on completion.

5.1.4 Where the property is leasehold and the property, or any building containing it, is insured by a reversioner or other third party, the seller is to use reasonable efforts to ensure that the insurance is maintained until completion and if, before completion, the property or building suffers loss or damage the seller is to assign to the buyer on completion, at the buyer's expense, such rights as the seller may have in the policy monies, in such form as the buyer reasonably requires.

5.1.5 If payment under a policy effected by or for the buyer is reduced, because the property is covered against loss or damage by an insurance policy effected by or on behalf of the seller, then, unless the seller is obliged to insure the property under condition 5.1.2, the purchase price is to be abated by the amount of that reduction.

5.1.6 Section 47 of the Law of Property Act 1925 does not apply.

5.2 **Occupation by buyer**

5.2.1 If the buyer is not already lawfully in the property, and the seller agrees to let him into occupation, the buyer occupies on the following terms.

5.2.2 The buyer is a licensee and not a tenant. The terms of the licence are that the buyer:

(a) cannot transfer it

(b) may permit members of his household to occupy the property

(c) is to pay or indemnify the seller against all outgoings and other expenses in respect of the property

(d) is to pay the seller a fee calculated at the contract rate on a sum equal to the purchase price (less any deposit paid) for the period of the licence

(e) is entitled to any rents and profits from any part of the property which he does not occupy

(f) is to keep the property in as good a state of repair as it was in when he went into occupation (except for fair wear and tear) and is not to alter it

(g) if the property is leasehold, is not to do anything which puts the seller in breach of his obligations in the lease, and

(h) is to quit the property when the licence ends.

5.2.3 The buyer is not in occupation for the purposes of this condition if he merely exercises rights of access given solely to do work agreed by the seller.

5.2.4 The buyer's licence ends on the earliest of: completion date, rescission of the contract or when five working days' notice given by one party to the other takes effect.

5.2.5 If the buyer is in occupation of the property after his licence has come to an end and the contract is subsequently completed he is to pay the seller compensation for his continued occupation calculated at the same rate as the fee mentioned in condition 5.2.2(d).

5.2.6 The buyer's right to raise requisitions is unaffected.

**6. COMPLETION**

6.1 **Date**

6.1.1 Completion date is twenty working days after the date of the contract but time is not of the essence of the contract unless a notice to complete has been served.

6.1.2 If the money due on completion is received after 2.00pm, completion is to be treated, for the purposes only of conditions 6.3 and 7.2, as taking place on the next working day as a result of the buyer's default.

6.1.3 Condition 6.1.2 does not apply and the seller is treated as in default if:

(a) the sale is with vacant possession of the property or any part of it, and

(b) the buyer is ready, able and willing to complete but does not pay the money due on completion until after 2.00pm because the seller has not vacated the property or that part by that time.

6.2 **Arrangements and place**

6.2.1 The buyer's conveyancer and the seller's conveyancer are to co-operate in agreeing arrangements for completing the contract.

6.2.2 Completion is to take place in England and Wales, either at the seller's conveyancer's office or at some other place which the seller reasonably specifies.

6.3 **Apportionments**

6.3.1 On evidence of proper payment being made, income and outgoings of the property are to be apportioned between the parties so far as the change of ownership on completion will affect entitlement to receive or liability to pay them.

6.3.2 If the whole property is sold with vacant possession or the seller exercises his option in condition 7.2.4, apportionment is to be made with effect from the date of actual completion; otherwise, it is to be made from completion date.

6.3.3 In apportioning any sum, it is to be assumed that the seller owns the property until the end of the day from which apportionment is made and that the sum accrues from day to day at the rate at which it is payable on that day.

6.3.4 For the purpose of apportioning income and outgoings, it is to be assumed that they accrue at an equal daily rate throughout the year.

6.3.5 When a sum to be apportioned is not known or easily ascertainable at completion, a provisional apportionment is to be made according to the best estimate available. As soon as the amount is known, a final apportionment is to be made and notified to the other party. Any resulting balance is to be paid no more than ten working days later, and if not then paid the balance is to bear interest at the contract rate from then until payment.

6.3.6 Compensation payable under condition 5.2.5 is not to be apportioned.

6.4 **Amount payable**

The amount payable by the buyer on completion is the purchase price and the contents price (less any deposit already paid to the seller or his agent) adjusted to take account of:

(a) apportionments made under condition 6.3

(b) any compensation to be paid or allowed under condition 7.2

(c) any sum payable under condition 5.1.3.

6.5 **Title deeds**

6.5.1 As soon as the buyer has complied with all his obligations under this contract o[n] completion the seller must hand over the documents of title.

6.5.2 Condition 6.5.1 does not apply to any documents of title relating to land being retained [by] the seller after completion.

6.6 **Rent receipts**

The buyer is to assume that whoever gave any receipt for a payment of rent or servic[e] charge which the seller produces was the person or the agent of the person then entitled [to] that rent or service charge.

6.7 **Means of payment**

The buyer is to pay the money due on completion by a direct transfer of cleared funds fro[m] an account held in the name of a conveyancer at a clearing bank and, if appropriate, a[n] unconditional release of a deposit held by a stakeholder.

6.8 **Notice to complete**

6.8.1 At any time after the time applicable under condition 6.1.2 on completion date, a party wh[o] is ready, able and willing to complete may give the other a notice to complete.

6.8.2 The parties are to complete the contract within ten working days of giving a notice t[o] complete, excluding the day on which the notice is given. For this purpose, time is of th[e] essence of the contract.

6.8.3 On receipt of a notice to complete:

(a) if the buyer paid no deposit, he is forthwith to pay a deposit of 10 per cent

(b) if the buyer paid a deposit of less than 10 per cent, he is forthwith to pay a furthe[r] deposit equal to the balance of that 10 per cent.

**7. REMEDIES**

7.1 **Errors and omissions**

7.1.1 If any plan or statement in the contract, or in the negotiations leading to it, is or wa[s] misleading or inaccurate due to an error or omission by the seller, the remedies availabl[e] to the buyer are as follows.

(a) When there is a material difference between the description or value of the property, [or] of any of the contents included in the contract, as represented and as it is, the buyer [is] entitled to damages.

(b) An error or omission only entitles the buyer to rescind the contract:

(i) where it results from fraud or recklessness, or

(ii) where he would be obliged, to his prejudice, to accept property differin[g] substantially (in quantity, quality or tenure) from what the error or omission ha[d] led him to expect.

7.1.2 If either party rescinds the contract:

(a) unless the rescission is a result of the buyer's breach of contract the deposit is to b[e] repaid to the buyer with accrued interest

(b) the buyer is to return any documents he received from the seller and is to cancel an[y] registration of the contract.

7.2 **Late completion**

7.2.1 If there is default by either or both of the parties in performing their obligations under th[e] contract and completion is delayed, the party whose total period of default is the greater i[s] to pay compensation to the other party.

7.2.2 Compensation is calculated at the contract rate on an amount equal to the purchase price less (where the buyer is the paying party) any deposit paid, for the period by which th[e] paying party's default exceeds that of the receiving party, or, if shorter, the period betwee[n] completion date and actual completion.

7.2.3 Any claim for loss resulting from delayed completion is to be reduced by an[y] compensation paid under this contract.

7.2.4 Where the buyer holds the property as tenant of the seller and completion is delayed, th[e] seller may give notice to the buyer, before the date of actual completion, that he intends t[o] take the net income from the property until completion. If he does so, he cannot clai[m] compensation under condition 7.2.1 as well.

7.3 **After completion**

Completion does not cancel liability to perform any outstanding obligation under this contract.

7.4 **Buyer's failure to comply with notice to complete**

7.4.1 If the buyer fails to complete in accordance with a notice to complete, the following terms apply.

7.4.2 The seller may rescind the contract, and if he does so:

(a) he may:

(i) forfeit and keep any deposit and accrued interest

(ii) resell the property and any contents included in the contract

(iii) claim damages

(b) the buyer is to return any documents he received from the seller and is to cancel an[y] registration of the contract.

7.4.3 The seller retains his other rights and remedies.

7.5 **Seller's failure to comply with notice to complete**

7.5.1 If the seller fails to complete in accordance with a notice to complete, the following terms apply.

7.5.2 The buyer may rescind the contract, and if he does so:

(a) the deposit is to be repaid to the buyer with accrued interest

(b) the buyer is to return any documents he received from the seller and is, at the seller's expense, to cancel any registration of the contract.

7.5.3 The buyer retains his other rights and remedies.

**8. LEASEHOLD PROPERTY**

8.1 **Existing leases**

8.1.1 The following provisions apply to a sale of leasehold land.

8.1.2 The seller having provided the buyer with copies of the documents embodying the lease terms, the buyer is treated as entering into the contract knowing and fully accepting those terms.

8.2 **New leases**

8.2.1 The following provisions apply to a contract to grant a new lease.

8.2.2 The conditions apply so that:

'seller' means the proposed landlord

'buyer' means the proposed tenant

'purchase price' means the premium to be paid on the grant of a lease.

8.2.3 The lease is to be in the form of the draft attached to the contract.

8.2.4 If the term of the new lease will exceed seven years, the seller is to deduce a title which will enable the buyer to register the lease at the Land Registry with an absolute title.

8.2.5 The seller is to engross the lease and a counterpart of it and is to send the counterpart to the buyer at least five working days before completion date.

8.2.6 The buyer is to execute the counterpart and deliver it to the seller on completion.

8.3 **Consent**

8.3.1 (a) The following provisions apply if a consent to let, assign or sub-let is required to complete the contract

(b) In this condition 'consent' means consent in the form which satisfies the requirement to obtain it.

8.3.2 (a) The seller is to apply for the consent at his expense, and to use all reasonable efforts to obtain it

(b) The buyer is to provide all information and references reasonably required.

8.3.3 Unless he is in breach of his obligation under condition 8.3.2, either party may rescind the contract by notice to the other party if three working days before completion date (or before a later date on which the parties have agreed to complete the contract):

(a) the consent has not been given, or

(b) the consent has been given subject to a condition to which a party reasonably objects. In that case, neither party is to be treated as in breach of contract and condition 7.1.2 applies.

**9. CONTENTS**

9.1 The following provisions apply to any contents which are included in the contract, whether or not a separate price is to be paid for them.

9.2 The contract takes effect as a contract for sale of goods.

9.3 The buyer takes the contents in the physical state they are in at the date of the contract.

9.4 Ownership of the contents passes to the buyer on actual completion.

## SPECIAL CONDITIONS

1.  (a) This contract incorporates the Standard Conditions of Sale (Fifth Edition – 2018 revision).

    (b) The terms used in this contract have the same meaning when used in the Conditions.

2.  Subject to the terms of this contract and to the Standard Conditions of Sale, the seller is to transfer the property with either full title guarantee or limited title guarantee, as specified on the front page.

3.  (a) The sale includes those contents which are indicated on the attached list as included in the sale and the buyer is to pay the contents price for them.

    (b) The sale excludes those fixtures which are at the property and are indicated on the attached list as excluded from the sale.

4.  The property is sold with vacant possession.

    (or)

4.  The property is sold subject to the following leases or tenancies:


5.  Conditions 6.1.2 & 6.1.3 shall take effect as if the time specified in them were [     ] rather than 2.00 pm.

6.  **Representations**

    Neither party can rely on any representation made by the other, unless made in writing by the other or his conveyancer, but this does not exclude liability for fraud or recklessness.

7.  **Occupier's consent**

    Each occupier identified below agrees with the seller and the buyer, in consideration of their entering into this contract, that the occupier concurs in the sale of the property on the terms of this contract, undertakes to vacate the property on or before the completion date and releases the property and any included fixtures and contents from any right or interest that the occupier may have.

    **Note:** this condition does not apply to occupiers under leases or tenancies subject to which the property is sold.

Names(s) and signature(s) of occupier(s) (if any):

Name

Signature

Notices may be sent to:

**Seller's conveyancer's name:**

   E-mail address:*

**Buyer's conveyancer's name:**

   E-mail address:*

*Adding an e-mail address authorises service by e-mail see condition 1.3.3(b)

\*   \*   \*

## ■ YOUR TURN

Have a go at answering question 1, remembering the guidance on pages 74–75:
- Refer to the structured approach in the SRA's assessment criteria on page 75.
- Create a list of the most important pieces of information to assist with drafting the contract.
- Timings are important: you will need to prepare and write your answer in 45 minutes.

---

**SQE1 Functioning legal knowledge link**

Remember from chapter 4 of *Revise SQE: Property Practice* that until contracts are exchanged, either party can withdraw from the transaction. Once contracts have been exchanged, they become legally binding.

---

## EVALUATING YOUR ANSWER

When you have attempted question 1, mark it yourself against the SQE2 legal drafting assessment criteria. Do you think your attempt met the threshold standard?

Now compare your attempt with the following key legal points and two sample answers to question 1. A circled number indicates that commentary is provided for this part of the answer. The commentary will explain whether or not the sample is likely to meet the threshold SQE2 standard.

---

➡**Key legal points: Question 1**

- Exchange of contracts is an important stage of a property purchase as this is where the sellers and buyers become bound to complete the transaction. Up until the point of exchange of contracts, either party can withdraw from the transaction without penalty.
- The contract and completion date should only be inserted upon exchange.
- When drafting contracts, it is important to be as specific as possible. You should utilise the office copy entries to ensure that the seller's name matches the contract. If there are any discrepancies, such as a name change, it is prudent to obtain evidence of this to provide to the buyer's solicitors, as they will raise this as a requisition on title. The Land Registry will require the names to match or evidence to support any changes before registering the new legal owners on the title.

# ■ SAMPLE ANSWER 1 TO QUESTION 1

## CONTRACT

**Incorporating the Standard Conditions of Sale (Fifth Edition – 2018 revision)**
© **The Law Society**

| For Conveyancer's use only |
|---|
| Buyer's conveyancer: _____ |
| Seller's conveyancer: _____ |
| Law Society Formula [A/B/C / Personal Exchange] |
| This information does not form part of the Contract |

**Date** : ①

**Seller** : Matthew Worthington of Franhurst Farm, Hurst Lane, Brumlington, Westshire, BLO 9HJ.

**Buyer** : Josef Christou and Doulla Christou of 44 Barry Street, Prestford, M25 OBA.

**Property (freehold/~~leasehold~~)** : Franhurst Farm, Hurst Lane, Brumlington, Westshire, BLO 9HJ.

**Title number/~~root of title~~** : L894332

**Specified incumbrances** : The covenants contained in entries 1 and 2 of the charges register of the title. ②

**Title guarantee (full/~~limited~~)** : Full

**Completion date** : ③

**Contract rate** : The Law Society's interest rate from time to time in force.

**Purchase price** : £305,000

**Deposit** : £30,500

**Contents price (if separate)** : £1,500 ④

**Balance** : £276,000

The seller will sell and the buyer will buy the property for the purchase price.

| WARNING | Signed |
|---|---|
| This is a formal document, designed to create legal rights and legal obligations. Take advice before using it. | |
| | Seller/Buyer |

# STANDARD CONDITIONS OF SALE (FIFTH EDITION - 2018 REVISION)
# (NATIONAL CONDITIONS OF SALE 25TH EDITION, LAW SOCIETY'S CONDITIONS OF SALE 2011)

**1. GENERAL**

**1.1 Definitions**

1.1.1 In these conditions:
- (a) 'accrued interest' means:
  - (i) if money has been placed on deposit or in a building society share account, the interest actually earned
  - (ii) otherwise, the interest which might reasonably have been earned by depositing the money at interest on seven days' notice of withdrawal with a clearing bank less, in either case, any proper charges for handling the money
- (b) 'clearing bank' means a bank admitted by the Bank of England as a direct participant in its CHAPS system
- (c) 'completion date' has the meaning given in condition 6.1.1
- (d) 'contents price' means any separate amount payable for contents included in the contract
- (e) 'contract rate' means the Law Society's interest rate from time to time in force
- (f) 'conveyancer' means a solicitor, barrister, duly certified notary public, licensed conveyancer or recognised body under sections 9 or 23 of the Administration of Justice Act 1985
- (g) 'lease' includes sub-lease, tenancy and agreement for a lease or sub-lease
- (h) 'mortgage' means a mortgage or charge securing the repayment of money
- (i) 'notice to complete' means a notice requiring completion of the contract in accordance with condition 6.8
- (j) 'public requirement' means any notice, order or proposal given or made (whether before or after the date of the contract) by a body acting on statutory authority
- (k) 'requisition' includes objection
- (l) 'transfer' includes conveyance and assignment
- (m) 'working day' means any day from Monday to Friday (inclusive) which is not Christmas Day, Good Friday or a statutory Bank Holiday.

1.1.2 In these conditions the terms 'absolute title' and 'official copies' have the special meanings given to them by the Land Registration Act 2002.

1.1.3 A party is ready, able and willing to complete:
- (a) if he could be, but for the default of the other party, and
- (b) in the case of the seller, even though the property remains subject to a mortgage, if the amount to be paid on completion enables the property to be transferred freed of all mortgages (except any to which the sale is expressly subject).

1.1.4 These conditions apply except as varied or excluded by the contract.

**1.2 Joint parties**

If there is more than one seller or more than one buyer, the obligations which they undertake can be enforced against them all jointly or against each individually.

**1.3 Notices and documents**

1.3.1 A notice required or authorised by the contract must be in writing.

1.3.2 Giving a notice or delivering a document to a party's conveyancer has the same effect as giving or delivering it to that party.

1.3.3 Where delivery of the original document is not essential, a notice or document is validly given or sent if it is sent:
- (a) by fax, or
- (b) by e-mail to an e-mail address for the intended recipient given in the contract

1.3.4 Subject to conditions 1.3.5 to 1.3.7, a notice is given and a document is delivered when it is received.

1.3.5
- (a) A notice or document sent through a document exchange is received when it is available for collection.
- (b) A notice or document which is received after 4.00pm on a working day, or on a day which is not a working day, is to be treated as having been received on the next working day.
- (c) An automated response to a notice or document sent by e-mail that the intended recipient is out of the office is to be treated as proof that the notice or document was not received.

1.3.6 Condition 1.3.7 applies unless there is proof:
- (a) that a notice or document has not been received, or
- (b) of when it was received.

1.3.7 A notice or document sent by the following means is treated as having been received as follows:

| | |
|---|---|
| (a) by first-class post: | before 4.00pm on the second working day after posting |
| (b) by second-class post: | before 4.00pm on the third working day after posting |
| (c) through a document exchange: | before 4.00pm on the first working day after the day on which it would normally be available for collection by the addressee |
| (d) by fax: | one hour after despatch |
| (e) by e-mail: | before 4.00pm on the first working day after despatch. |

**1.4 VAT**

1.4.1 The purchase price and the contents price are inclusive of any value added tax.

1.4.2 All other sums made payable by the contract are exclusive of any value added tax and where a supply is made which is chargeable to value added tax, the recipient of the supply is to pay the supplier (in addition to any other amounts payable under the contract) a sum equal to the value added tax chargeable on that supply.

**1.5 Assignment and sub-sales**

1.5.1 The buyer is not entitled to transfer the benefit of the contract

1.5.2 The seller cannot be required to transfer the property in parts or to any person other than the buyer.

**1.6 Third party rights**

Unless otherwise expressly stated nothing in this contract will create rights pursuant to the Contracts (Rights of Third Parties) Act 1999 in favour of anyone other than the parties to the contract.

**2. FORMATION**

**2.1 Date**

2.1.1 If the parties intend to make a contract by exchanging duplicate copies by post or through a document exchange, the contract is made when the last copy is posted or deposited at the document exchange.

2.1.2 If the parties' conveyancers agree to treat exchange as taking place before duplicate copies are actually exchanged, the contract is made as so agreed.

**2.2 Deposit**

2.2.1 The buyer is to pay or send a deposit of 10 per cent of the purchase price no later than the date of the contract.

2.2.2 If a cheque tendered in payment of all or part of the deposit is dishonoured when first presented, the seller may, within seven working days of being notified that the cheque has been dishonoured, give notice to the buyer that the contract is discharged by the buyer's breach.

2.2.3 Conditions 2.2.4 to 2.2.6 do not apply on a sale by auction.

2.2.4 The deposit is to be paid:
- (a) by electronic means from an account held in the name of a conveyancer at a clearing bank to an account in the name of the seller's conveyancer or (in a case where condition 2.2.5 applies) a conveyancer nominated by him and maintained at a clearing bank or
- (b) to the seller's conveyancer or (in a case where condition 2.2.5 applies) a conveyancer nominated by him by cheque drawn on a solicitor's or licensed conveyancer's client account

2.2.5 If before completion date the seller agrees to buy another property in England and Wales for his residence, he may use all or any part of the deposit as a deposit in that transaction to be held on terms to the same effect as this condition and condition 2.2.6.

2.2.6 Any deposit or part of a deposit not being used in accordance with condition 2.2.5 is to be held by the seller's conveyancer as stakeholder on terms that on completion it is paid to the seller with accrued interest.

**2.3 Auctions**

2.3.1 On a sale by auction the following conditions apply to the property and, if it is sold in lots, to each lot.

2.3.2 The sale is subject to a reserve price.

2.3.3 The seller, or a person on his behalf, may bid up to the reserve price

2.3.4 The auctioneer may refuse any bid.

2.3.5 If there is a dispute about a bid, the auctioneer may resolve the dispute or restart the auction at the last undisputed bid.

2.3.6 The deposit is to be paid to the auctioneer as agent for the seller.

**3. MATTERS AFFECTING THE PROPERTY**

**3.1 Freedom from incumbrances**

3.1.1 The seller is selling the property free from incumbrances, other than those mentioned in condition 3.1.2.

3.1.2 The incumbrances subject to which the property is sold are:
- (a) those specified in the contract
- (b) those discoverable by inspection of the property before the date of the contract.
- (c) those the seller does not and could not reasonably know about
- (d) those, other than mortgages, which the buyer knows about
- (e) entries made before the date of the contract in any public register except th maintained by the Land Registry or its Land Charges Department or by Compa House
- (f) public requirements.

3.1.3 After the contract is made, the seller is to give the buyer written details without delay of new public requirement and of anything in writing which he learns about concernir matter covered by condition 3.1.2.

3.1.4 The buyer is to bear the cost of complying with any outstanding public requirement and indemnify the seller against any liability resulting from a public requirement.

**3.2 Physical state**

3.2.1 The buyer accepts the property in the physical state it is in at the date of the contract un the seller is building or converting it.

3.2.2 A leasehold property is sold subject to any subsisting breach of a condition or tena obligation relating to the physical state of the property which renders the lease liabl forfeiture.

3.2.3 A sub-lease is granted subject to any subsisting breach of a condition or tenant's obliga relating to the physical state of the property which renders the seller's own lease liab forfeiture.

**3.3 Leases affecting the property**

3.3.1 The following provisions apply if any part of the property is sold subject to a lease.

3.3.2
- (a) The seller having provided the buyer with full details of each lease or copies of documents embodying the lease terms, the buyer is treated as entering into contract knowing and fully accepting those terms.
- (b) The seller is to inform the buyer without delay if the lease ends or if the seller learn any application by the tenant in connection with the lease; the seller is then to ac the buyer reasonably directs, and the buyer is to indemnify him against all consequ loss and expense.
- (c) Except with the buyer's consent, the seller is not to agree to any proposal to cha the lease terms nor to take any step to end the lease.
- (d) The seller is to inform the buyer without delay of any change to the lease terms wh may be proposed or agreed.
- (e) The buyer is to indemnify the seller against all claims arising from the lease after ac completion; this includes claims which are unenforceable against a buyer for war registration.
- (f) The seller takes no responsibility for what rent is lawfully recoverable, nor for whe or how any legislation affects the lease.
- (g) If the let land is not wholly within the property, the seller may apportion the re

**4. TITLE AND TRANSFER**

**4.1 Proof of title**

4.1.1 Without cost to the buyer, the seller is to provide the buyer with proof of the title to property and of his ability to transfer it, or to procure its transfer.

4.1.2 Where the property has a registered title the proof is to include official copies of the ite referred to in rules 134(1)(a) and (b) and 135(1)(a) of the Land Registration Rules 2003 far as they are not to be discharged or overridden at or before completion.

4.1.3 Where the property has an unregistered title, the proof is to include:
- (a) an abstract of title or an epitome of title with photocopies of the documents, a
- (b) production of every document or an abstract, epitome or copy of it with an orig marking by a conveyancer either against the original or an examined abstract or examined copy.

**4.2 Requisitions**

4.2.1 The buyer may not raise requisitions:
- (a) on any title shown by the seller before the contract was made
- (b) in relation to the matters covered by condition 3.1.2.

4.2.2 Notwithstanding condition 4.2.1, the buyer may, within six working days of a matter com to his attention after the contract was made, raise written requisitions on that matter. In t event, steps 3 and 4 in condition 4.3.1 apply.

4.2.3 On the expiry of the relevant time limit under condition 4.2.2 or condition 4.3.1, the bu loses his right to raise requisitions or to make observations.

**4.3 Timetable**

4.3.1 Subject to condition 4.2 and to the extent that the seller did not take the steps describe condition 4.1.1 before the contract was made, the following are the steps for deducing a investigating the title to the property to be taken within the following time lim

| Step | Time Limit |
|---|---|
| 1. The seller is to comply with condition 4.1.1 | Immediately after making the contract |
| 2. The buyer may raise written requisitions | Six working days after either the date of contract or the date of delivery of the sell evidence of title on which the requisitions raised, whichever is the later |
| 3. The seller is to reply in writing to any requisitions raised | Four working days after receiving t requisitions |
| 4. The buyer may make written observations on the seller's replies | Three working days after receiving the repl |

The time limit on the buyer's right to raise requisitions applies even where the se supplies incomplete evidence of his title, but the buyer may, within six working days fr delivery of any further evidence, raise further requisitions resulting from that eviden

4.3.2 The parties are to take the following steps to prepare and agree the transfer of the prope within the following time limits:

| Step | Time Limit |
|---|---|
| A. The buyer is to send the seller a draft transfer | At least twelve working days befo completion date |
| B. The seller is to approve or revise that draft and either return it or retain it for use as the actual transfer | Four working days after delivery of the d transfer |
| C. If the draft is returned the buyer is to send an engrossment to the seller | At least five working days before complet date |

4.3.3 Periods of time under conditions 4.3.1 and 4.3.2 may run concurrently.

4.3.4 If the period between the date of the contract and completion date is less than 15 work days, the time limits in conditions 4.2.2, 4.3.1 and 4.3.2 are to be reduced by the sa proportion as that period bears to the period of 15 working days. Fractions of a working are to be rounded down except that the time limit to perform any step is not to be less th one working day.

**4.4 Defining the property**

The seller need not:
- (a) prove the exact boundaries of the property
- (b) prove who owns fences, ditches, hedges or walls
- (c) separately identify parts of the property with different titles further than he may be a to do from information in his possession.

**4.5 Rents and rentcharges**

The fact that a rent or rentcharge, whether payable or receivable by the owner of t property, has been, or will on completion be, informally apportioned is not to be regarded a defect in title.

**4.6 Transfer**

4.6.1 The buyer does not prejudice his right to raise requisitions, or to require replies to a raised, by taking any steps in relation to preparing or agreeing the transfe

4.6.2 Subject to condition 4.6.3, the seller is to transfer the property with full title guarante

4.6.3 The transfer is to have effect as if the disposition is expressly made subject to all matters covered by condition 3.1.2 and, if the property is leasehold, is to contain a statement that the covenants set out in section 4 of the Law of Property (Miscellaneous Provisions) Act 1994 will not extend to any breach of the tenant's covenants in the lease relating to the physical state of the property.

4.6.4 If after completion the seller will remain bound by any obligation affecting the property which was disclosed to the buyer before the contract was made, but the law does not imply any covenant by the buyer to indemnify the seller against liability for future breaches of it:
   (a)  the buyer is to covenant in the transfer to indemnify the seller against liability for any future breach of the obligation and to perform it from then on, and
   (b)  if required by the seller, the buyer is to execute and deliver to the seller on completion a duplicate transfer prepared by the buyer.

4.6.5 The seller is to arrange at his expense that, in relation to every document of title which the buyer does not receive on completion, the buyer is to have the benefit of:
   (a)  a written acknowledgement of his right to its production, and
   (b)  a written undertaking for its safe custody (except while it is held by a mortgagee or by someone in a fiduciary capacity).

4.7 **Membership of company**
Where the seller is, or is required to be, a member of a company that has an interest in the property or has management responsibilities for the property or the surrounding areas, the seller is, without cost to the buyer, to provide such documents on completion as will enable the buyer to become a member of that company.

5. **RISK, INSURANCE AND OCCUPATION PENDING COMPLETION**
5.1.1 The property is at the risk of the buyer from the date of the contract
5.1.2 The seller is under no obligation to the buyer to insure the property unless:
   (a)  the contract provides that a policy effected by or for the seller and insuring the property or any part of it against liability for loss or damage is to continue in force, or
   (b)  the property or any part of it is let on terms under which the seller (whether as landlord or as tenant) is obliged to insure against loss or damage.

5.1.3 If the seller is obliged to insure the property under condition 5.1.2, the seller is to:
   (a)  do everything necessary to maintain the policy
   (b)  permit the buyer to inspect the policy or evidence of its terms
   (c)  if before completion the property suffers loss or damage:
     (i)  pay to the buyer on completion the amount of the policy monies which the seller has received, so far as not applied in repairing or reinstating the property, and
     (ii)  if no final payment has then been received, assign to the buyer, at the buyer's expense, all rights to claim under the policy in such form as the buyer reasonably requires and pending execution of the assignment hold any policy monies received in trust for the buyer
   (d)  cancel the policy on completion.

5.1.4 Where the property is leasehold and the property, or any building containing it, is insured by a reversioner or other third party, the seller is to use reasonable efforts to ensure that the insurance is maintained until completion and if, before completion, the property or building suffers loss or damage the seller is to assign to the buyer on completion, at the buyer's expense, such rights as the seller may have in the policy monies, in such form as the buyer reasonably requires.

5.1.5 If payment under a policy effected by or for the buyer is reduced, because the property is covered against loss or damage by an insurance policy effected by or on behalf of the seller, then, unless the seller is obliged to insure the property under condition 5.1.2, the purchase price is to be abated by the amount of that reduction.

5.1.6 Section 47 of the Law of Property Act 1925 does not apply.

5.2 **Occupation by buyer**
5.2.1 If the buyer is not already lawfully in the property, and the seller agrees to let him into occupation, the buyer occupies on the following terms.
5.2.2 The buyer is a licensee and not a tenant. The terms of the licence are that the buyer:
   (a)  cannot transfer it
   (b)  may permit members of his household to occupy the property
   (c)  is to pay or indemnify the seller against all outgoings and other expenses in respect of the property
   (d)  is to pay the seller a fee calculated at the contract rate on a sum equal to the purchase price (less any deposit paid) for the period of the licence
   (e)  is entitled to any rents and profits from any part of the property which he does not occupy
   (f)  is to keep the property in as good a state of repair as it was in when he went into occupation (except for fair wear and tear) and is not to alter it
   (g)  if the property is leasehold, is not to do anything which puts the seller in breach of his obligations in the lease, and
   (h)  is to quit the property when the licence ends.

5.2.3 The buyer is not in occupation for the purposes of this condition if he merely exercises rights of access given solely to do work agreed by the seller.
5.2.4 The buyer's licence ends on the earliest of: completion date, rescission of the contract or when five working days' notice given by one party to the other takes effect.
5.2.5 If the buyer is in occupation of the property after his licence has come to an end and the contract is subsequently completed he is to pay the seller compensation for his continued occupation calculated at the same rate as the fee mentioned in condition 5.2.2(d).
5.2.6 The buyer's right to raise requisitions is unaffected.

6. **COMPLETION**
6.1 **Date**
6.1.1 Completion date is twenty working days after the date of the contract but time is not of the essence of the contract unless a notice to complete has been served.
6.1.2 If the money due on completion is received after 2.00pm, completion is to be treated, for the purposes only of conditions 6.3 and 7.2, as taking place on the next working day as a result of the buyer's default.
6.1.3 Condition 6.1.2 does not apply and the seller is treated as in default if:
   (a)  the sale is with vacant possession of the property or any part of it, and
   (b)  the buyer is ready, able and willing to complete but does not pay the money due on completion until after 2.00pm because the seller has not vacated the property or that part by that time.

6.2 **Arrangements and place**
6.2.1 The buyer's conveyancer and the seller's conveyancer are to co-operate in agreeing arrangements for completing the contract.
6.2.2 Completion is to take place in England and Wales, either at the seller's conveyancer's office or at some other place which the seller reasonably specifies.

6.3 **Apportionments**
6.3.1 On evidence of proper payment being made, income and outgoings of the property are to be apportioned between the parties so far as the change of ownership on completion will affect entitlement to receive or liability to pay them.
6.3.2 If the whole property is sold with vacant possession or the seller exercises his option in condition 7.2.4, apportionment is to be made with effect from the date of actual completion; otherwise, it is to be made from completion date.
6.3.3 In apportioning any sum, it is to be assumed that the seller owns the property until the end of the day from which apportionment is made and that the sum accrues from day to day at the rate at which it is payable on that day.
6.3.4 For the purpose of apportioning income and outgoings, it is to be assumed that they accrue at an equal daily rate throughout the year.
6.3.5 When a sum to be apportioned is not known or easily ascertainable at completion, a provisional apportionment is to be made according to the best estimate available. As soon as the amount is known, a final apportionment is to be made and notified to the other party. Any resulting balance is to be paid no more than ten working days later, and if not then paid the balance is to bear interest at the contract rate from then until payment.
6.3.6 Compensation payable under condition 5.2.5 is not to be apportioned.

6.4 **Amount payable**
The amount payable by the buyer on completion is the purchase price and the contents price (less any deposit already paid to the seller or his agent) adjusted to take account of:
   (a)  apportionments made under condition 6.3
   (b)  any compensation to be paid or allowed under condition 7.2
   (c)  any sum payable under condition 5.1.3.

6.5 **Title deeds**
6.5.1 As soon as the buyer has complied with all his obligations under this contract on completion the seller must hand over the documents of title.
6.5.2 Condition 6.5.1 does not apply to any documents of title relating to land being retained by the seller after completion.

6.6 **Rent receipts**
The buyer is to assume that whoever gave any receipt for a payment of rent or service charge which the seller produces was the person or the agent of the person then entitled to that rent or service charge.

6.7 **Means of payment**
The buyer is to pay the money due on completion by a direct transfer of cleared funds from an account held in the name of a conveyancer at a clearing bank and, if appropriate, an unconditional release of a deposit held by a stakeholder.

6.8 **Notice to complete**
6.8.1 At any time after the time applicable under condition 6.1.2 on completion date, a party who is ready, able and willing to complete may give the other a notice to complete.
6.8.2 The parties are to complete the contract within ten working days of giving a notice to complete, excluding the day on which the notice is given. For this purpose, time is of the essence of the contract.
6.8.3 On receipt of a notice to complete:
   (a)  if the buyer paid no deposit, he is forthwith to pay a deposit of 10 per cent
   (b)  if the buyer paid a deposit of less than 10 per cent, he is forthwith to pay a further deposit equal to the balance of that 10 per cent.

7. **REMEDIES**
7.1 **Errors and omissions**
7.1.1 If any plan or statement in the contract, or in the negotiations leading to it, is or was misleading or inaccurate due to an error or omission by the seller, the remedies available to the buyer are as follows.
   (a)  When there is a material difference between the description or value of the property, or of any of the contents included in the contract, as represented and as it is, the buyer is entitled to damages.
   (b)  An error or omission only entitles the buyer to rescind the contract:
     (i)  where it results from fraud or recklessness, or
     (ii)  where he would be obliged, to his prejudice, to accept property differing substantially (in quantity, quality or tenure) from what the error or omission had led him to expect.

7.1.2 If either party rescinds the contract:
   (a)  unless the rescission is a result of the buyer's breach of contract the deposit is to be repaid to the buyer with accrued interest
   (b)  the buyer is to return any documents he received from the seller and is to cancel any registration of the contract.

7.2 **Late completion**
7.2.1 If there is default by either or both of the parties in performing their obligations under the contract and completion is delayed, the party whose total period of default is the greater is to pay compensation to the other party.
7.2.2 Compensation is calculated at the contract rate on an amount equal to the purchase price, less (where the buyer is the paying party) any deposit paid, for the period by which the paying party's default exceeds that of the receiving party, or, if shorter, the period between completion date and actual completion.
7.2.3 Any claim for loss resulting from delayed completion is to be reduced by any compensation paid under this contract.
7.2.4 Where the buyer holds the property as tenant of the seller and completion is delayed, the seller may give notice to the buyer, before the date of actual completion, that he intends to take the net income from the property until completion. If he does so, he cannot claim compensation under condition 7.2.1 as well.

7.3 **After completion**
Completion does not cancel liability to perform any outstanding obligation under this contract.

7.4 **Buyer's failure to comply with notice to complete**
7.4.1 If the buyer fails to complete in accordance with a notice to complete, the following terms apply.
7.4.2 The seller may rescind the contract, and if he does so:
   (a)  he may:
     (i)  forfeit and keep any deposit and accrued interest
     (ii)  resell the property and any contents included in the contract
     (iii)  claim damages
   (b)  the buyer is to return any documents he received from the seller and is to cancel any registration of the contract.

7.4.3 The seller retains his other rights and remedies.

7.5 **Seller's failure to comply with notice to complete**
7.5.1 If the seller fails to complete in accordance with a notice to complete, the following terms apply.
7.5.2 The buyer may rescind the contract, and if he does so:
   (a)  the deposit is to be repaid to the buyer with accrued interest
   (b)  the buyer is to return any documents he received from the seller and is, at the seller's expense, to cancel any registration of the contract.

7.5.3 The buyer retains his other rights and remedies.

8. **LEASEHOLD PROPERTY**
8.1 **Existing leases**
8.1.1 The following provisions apply to a sale of leasehold land.
8.1.2 The seller having provided the buyer with copies of the documents embodying the lease terms, the buyer is treated as entering into the contract knowing and fully accepting those terms.

8.2 **New leases**
8.2.1 The following provisions apply to a contract to grant a new lease.
8.2.2 The conditions apply so that:
'seller' means the proposed landlord
'buyer' means the proposed tenant
'purchase price' means the premium to be paid on the grant of a lease.
8.2.3 The lease is to be in the form of the draft attached to the contract.
8.2.4 If the term of the new lease will exceed seven years, the seller is to deduce a title which will enable the buyer to register the lease at the Land Registry with an absolute title.
8.2.5 The seller is to engross the lease and a counterpart of it and is to send the counterpart to the buyer at least five working days before completion date.
8.2.6 The buyer is to execute the counterpart and deliver it to the seller on completion.

8.3 **Consent**
8.3.1   (a)  The following provisions apply if a consent to let, assign or sub-let is required to complete the contract
   (b)  In this condition 'consent' means consent in the form which satisfies the requirement to obtain it.
8.3.2   (a)  The seller is to apply for the consent at his expense, and to use all reasonable efforts to obtain it
   (b)  The buyer is to provide all information and references reasonably required.
8.3.3 Unless he is in breach of his obligation under condition 8.3.2, either party may rescind the contract by notice to the other party if three working days before completion date (or before a later date on which the parties have agreed to complete the contract):
   (a)  the consent has not been given, or
   (b)  the consent has been given subject to a condition to which a party reasonably objects. In that case, neither party is to be treated as in breach of contract and condition 7.1.2 applies.

9. **CONTENTS**
9.1 The following provisions apply to any contents which are included in the contract, whether or not a separate price is to be paid for them.
9.2 The contract takes effect as a contract for sale of goods.
9.3 The buyer takes the contents in the physical state they are in at the date of the contract.
9.4 Ownership of the contents passes to the buyer on actual completion.

## SPECIAL CONDITIONS

1.  (a) This contract incorporates the Standard Conditions of Sale (Fifth Edition – 2018 revision).
    (b) The terms used in this contract have the same meaning when used in the Conditions.
2.  Subject to the terms of this contract and to the Standard Conditions of Sale, the seller is to transfer the property with either full title guarantee or limited title guarantee, as specified on the front page.
3.  (a) The sale includes those contents which are indicated on the attached list as included in the sale and the buyer is to pay the contents price for them.
    (b) The sale excludes those fixtures which are at the property and are indicated on the attached list as excluded from the sale.
4.  The property is sold with vacant possession.
(or)
4.  ~~The property is sold subject to the following leases or tenancies:~~ ⑤
5.  Conditions 6.1.2 & 6.1.3 shall take effect as if the time specified in them were [      ] pm. ⑥
6.  **Representations**
    Neither party can rely on any representation made by the other, unless made in writing by the other or his conveyancer, but this does not exclude liability for fraud or recklessness.
7.  **Occupier's consent**
    Each occupier identified below agrees with the seller and the buyer, in consideration of their entering into this contract, that the occupier concurs in the sale of the property on the terms of this contract, undertakes to vacate the property on or before the completion date and releases the property and any included fixtures and contents from any right or interest that the occupier may have.
    **Note:** this condition does not apply to occupiers under leases or tenancies subject to which the property is sold.

Names(s) and signature(s) of occupier(s) (if any):
Name Daniella Worthington ⑦
Signature

Notices may be sent to:
**Seller's conveyancer's name:**

   E-mail address:*

**Buyer's conveyancer's name:**

Star Legal

   E-mail address:*

*Adding an e-mail address authorises service by e-mail see condition 1.3.3(b).

# COMMENTARY

① The contract should not be dated until exchange of contracts takes place. The reason for this is that the day for exchange could vary, and you could end up with numerous corrections needing to be signed.

② It is imperative to make reference to anything that the future owner(s) of the property will be burdened by. In this instance, there are two entries in the charges register that will effectively run with the land and will therefore bind the future owners. Note that any mortgages that are to be discharged upon completion do not need to be referred to in this section.

③ No completion date should be inserted until exchange of contracts takes place. Although clients may have an ideal date that they wish to complete, it is not possible in the initial stages to offer this definitively. It is important to manage client expectations with this issue to avoid their dissatisfaction.

④ The contract should incorporate any chattels that have been agreed between the parties to be purchased. The instructions clearly state that the client is selling the sofa for an additional £1,500. This shows the examiner that the candidate is utilising the information provided and drafting a document which is legally comprehensive. If this was omitted, there could potentially be a problem: the client might leave the sofa, but the buyers do not pay the additional £1,500. This could result in a professional negligence claim being made against the firm.

⑤ One option will need to be crossed through. If clients are purchasing the property with the intention of moving into it, it should read that the property is sold subject to vacant possession, meaning that there will be no one remaining in the property when completion has taken place. The only time vacant possession should be crossed through would be if the property was being purchased with tenants in situ (as a buy to let property).

⑥ In condition 6.1.2, the usual time for completion is stated as 2pm. When you have a sale and purchase that is taking place on the same day, these will usually be synchronised. This is where you would need to vary the times so that your client does not end up with no property or two properties. The sale completion time should always be earlier than the purchase completion time. This will allow for enough time to transfer the money received for the sale, to the purchasers' solicitors. If both the sale and purchase completion times were the same, for example 2 PM, you could encounter a problem if the money from the sale came in at 1.59 PM (still in time for completion) but then could not get the monies over to the purchase within 1 minute. This would result in your client being accountable for delayed completion compensation, through no fault of their own. Varying the times – such as 1 PM for the sale and 2 PM for the purchase – prevents this issue.

⑦ The client has a child over the age of 18 who is currently residing in the property. Daniella could claim to have a beneficial interest in the property if she could evidence contributions made. It is therefore necessary for all occupants over the age of 18 to sign the contract as an occupier to confirm that they will vacate the property upon completion. This prevents them from being able to claim an overriding interest in the property, which may not be extinguished upon the sale of the property (if overreaching has not taken place).

## Does this answer meet the threshold?

The sample answer above includes all of the components that a contract requires in order to be legally binding. It adequately protects the buyers in the event of the daughter not moving out by including her as an occupier in the contract. This will ensure that she does not have any overriding interest in the property upon completion and will ensure vacant possession for the buyers. It is therefore likely to meet the threshold standard for SQE2 legal drafting.

Now consider the second sample answer to question 1.

# ■ SAMPLE ANSWER 2 TO QUESTION 1

## CONTRACT
**Incorporating the Standard Conditions of Sale (Fifth Edition – 2018 revision)**
© **The Law Society**

> ──── For Conveyancer's use only ────
> Buyer's conveyancer: _____
> Seller's conveyancer: _____
> Law Society Formula [A/B/C / Personal Exchange]
> This information does not form part of the
> Contract

| | |
|---|---|
| **Date** | : |
| **Seller** | : Matthew Worthington of Franhurst Farm, Hurst Lane, Brumlington, Westshire, BLO 9HJ. |
| **Buyer** | : Josef Christou and Doulla Christou of 44 Barry Street, Prestford, M25 0BA. |
| **Property (freehold/~~leasehold~~)** | : Franhurst Farm, Hurst Lane, Brumlington, Westshire, BLO 9HJ. |
| **Title number/~~root of title~~** | : L894332 |
| **Specified incumbrances** | : None ❶ |
| **Title guarantee (full/~~limited~~)** | : Full |
| **Completion date** | : 29th October 202# ❷ |
| **Contract rate** | : 6% above the base rate of Barclays Bank Plc ❸ |
| **Purchase price** | : £305,000 |
| **Deposit** | : £30,500 |
| **Contents price (if separate)** | : ❹ |
| **Balance** | : £276,000 |

The seller will sell and the buyer will buy the property for the purchase price.

| WARNING | Signed |
|---|---|
| This is a formal document, designed to create legal rights and legal obligations. Take advice before using it. | Seller/Buyer |

# STANDARD CONDITIONS OF SALE (FIFTH EDITION - 2018 REVISION)
## (NATIONAL CONDITIONS OF SALE 25TH EDITION, LAW SOCIETY'S CONDITIONS OF SALE 2011)

## GENERAL

### Definitions

In these conditions:
(a) 'accrued interest' means:
  (i) if money has been placed on deposit or in a building society share account, the interest actually earned
  (ii) otherwise, the interest which might reasonably have been earned by depositing the money at interest on seven days' notice of withdrawal with a clearing bank less, in either case, any proper charges for handling the money
(b) 'clearing bank' means a bank admitted by the Bank of England as a direct participant in its CHAPS system
(c) 'completion date' has the meaning given in condition 6.1.1
(d) 'contents price' means any separate amount payable for contents included in the contract
(e) 'contract rate' means the Law Society's interest rate from time to time in force
(f) 'conveyancer' means a solicitor, barrister, duly certified notary public, licensed conveyancer or recognised body under sections 9 or 23 of the Administration of Justice Act 1985
(g) 'lease' includes sub-lease, tenancy and agreement for a lease or sub-lease
(h) 'mortgage' means a mortgage or charge securing the repayment of money
(i) 'notice to complete' means a notice requiring completion of the contract in accordance with condition 6.8
(j) 'public requirement' means any notice, order or proposal given or made (whether before or after the date of the contract) by a body acting on statutory authority
(k) 'requisition' includes objection
(l) 'transfer' includes conveyance and assignment
(m) 'working day' means any day from Monday to Friday (inclusive) which is not Christmas Day, Good Friday or a statutory Bank Holiday.

In these conditions the terms 'absolute title' and 'official copies' have the special meanings given to them by the Land Registration Act 2002.

A party is ready, able and willing to complete:
(a) if he could be, but for the default of the other party, and
(b) in the case of the seller, even though the property remains subject to a mortgage, if the amount to be paid on completion enables the property to be transferred freed of all mortgages (except any to which the sale is expressly subject).

These conditions apply except as varied or excluded by the contract.

### Joint parties

If there is more than one seller or more than one buyer, the obligations which they undertake can be enforced against them all jointly or against each individually.

### Notices and documents

A notice required or authorised by the contract must be in writing.

Giving a notice or delivering a document to a party's conveyancer has the same effect as giving or delivering it to that party.

Where delivery of the original document is not essential, a notice or document is validly given or sent if it is sent:
(a) by fax, or
(b) by e-mail to an e-mail address for the intended recipient given in the contract

Subject to conditions 1.3.5 to 1.3.7, a notice is given and a document is delivered when it is received.
(a) A notice or document sent through a document exchange is received when it is available for collection.
(b) A notice or document which is received after 4.00pm on a working day, or on a day which is not a working day, is to be treated as having been received on the next working day.
(c) An automated response to a notice or document sent by e-mail that the intended recipient is out of the office is to be treated as proof that the notice or document was not received.

Condition 1.3.7 applies unless there is proof:
(a) that a notice or document has not been received, or
(b) of when it was received.

A notice or document sent by the following means is treated as having been received as follows:

| | |
|---|---|
| (a) by first-class post: | before 4.00pm on the second working day after posting |
| (b) by second-class post: | before 4.00pm on the third working day after posting |
| (c) through a document exchange: | before 4.00pm on the first working day after the day on which it would normally be available for collection by the addressee |
| (d) by fax: | one hour after despatch |
| (e) by e-mail: | before 4.00pm on the first working day after despatch. |

### VAT

The purchase price and the contents price are inclusive of any value added tax.

All other sums made payable by the contract are exclusive of any value added tax and where a supply is made which is chargeable to value added tax, the recipient of the supply is to pay the supplier (in addition to any other amounts payable under the contract) a sum equal to the value added tax chargeable on that supply.

### Assignment and sub-sales

The buyer is not entitled to transfer the benefit of the contract

The seller cannot be required to transfer the property in parts or to any person other than the buyer.

### Third party rights

Unless otherwise expressly stated nothing in this contract will create rights pursuant to the Contracts (Rights of Third Parties) Act 1999 in favour of anyone other than the parties to the contract.

## FORMATION

### Date

If the parties intend to make a contract by exchanging duplicate copies by post or through a document exchange, the contract is made when the last copy is posted or deposited at the document exchange.

If the parties' conveyancers agree to treat exchange as taking place before duplicate copies are actually exchanged, the contract is made as so agreed.

### Deposit

The buyer is to pay or send a deposit of 10 per cent of the purchase price no later than the date of the contract.

If a cheque tendered in payment of all or part of the deposit is dishonoured when first presented, the seller may, within seven working days of being notified that the cheque has been dishonoured, give notice to the buyer that the contract is discharged by the buyer's breach.

Conditions 2.2.4 to 2.2.6 do not apply on a sale by auction.

The deposit is to be paid:
(a) by electronic means from an account held in the name of a conveyancer at a clearing bank to an account in the name of the seller's conveyancer or (in a case where condition 2.2.5 applies) a conveyancer nominated by him and maintained at a clearing bank or
(b) to the seller's conveyancer or (in a case where condition 2.2.5 applies) a conveyancer nominated by him by cheque drawn on a solicitor's or licensed conveyancer's client account

If before completion date the seller agrees to buy another property in England and Wales for his residence, he may use all or any part of the deposit as a deposit in that transaction to be held on terms to the same effect as this condition and condition 2.2.6.

Any deposit or part of a deposit not being used in accordance with condition 2.2.5 is to be held by the seller's conveyancer as stakeholder on terms that on completion it is paid to the seller with accrued interest.

### Auctions

On a sale by auction the following conditions apply to the property and, if it is sold in lots, to each lot.

The sale is subject to a reserve price.

The seller, or a person on his behalf, may bid up to the reserve price.

The auctioneer may refuse any bid.

If there is a dispute about a bid, the auctioneer may resolve the dispute or restart the auction at the last undisputed bid.

The deposit is to be paid to the auctioneer as agent for the seller.

## 3. MATTERS AFFECTING THE PROPERTY

### 3.1 Freedom from incumbrances

3.1.1 The seller is selling the property free from incumbrances, other than those mentioned in condition 3.1.2.

3.1.2 The incumbrances subject to which the property is sold are:
(a) those specified in the contract
(b) those discoverable by inspection of the property before the date of the contract.
(c) those the seller does not and could not reasonably know about
(d) those, other than mortgages, which the buyer knows about
(e) entries made before the date of the contract in any public register except those maintained by the Land Registry or its Land Charges Department or by Companies House
(f) public requirements.

3.1.3 After the contract is made, the seller is to give the buyer written details without delay of any new public requirement and of anything in writing which he learns about concerning a matter covered by condition 3.1.2.

3.1.4 The buyer is to bear the cost of complying with any outstanding public requirement and is to indemnify the seller against any liability resulting from a public requirement.

### 3.2 Physical state

3.2.1 The buyer accepts the property in the physical state it is in at the date of the contract unless the seller is building or converting it.

3.2.2 A leasehold property is sold subject to any subsisting breach of a condition or tenant's obligation relating to the physical state of the property which renders the lease liable to forfeiture.

3.2.3 A sub-lease is granted subject to any subsisting breach of a condition or tenant's obligation relating to the physical state of the property which renders the seller's own lease liable to forfeiture.

### 3.3 Leases affecting the property

3.3.1 The following provisions apply if any part of the property is sold subject to a lease.

3.3.2 (a) The seller having provided the buyer with full details of each lease or copies of the documents embodying the lease terms, the buyer is treated as entering into the contract knowing and fully accepting those terms.
(b) The seller is to inform the buyer without delay if the lease ends or if the seller learns of any application by the tenant in connection with the lease; the seller is then to act as the buyer reasonably directs, and the buyer is to indemnify him against all consequent loss and expense.
(c) Except with the buyer's consent, the seller is not to agree to any proposal to change the lease terms nor to take any step to end the lease.
(d) The seller is to inform the buyer without delay of any change to the lease terms which may be proposed or agreed.
(e) The buyer is to indemnify the seller against all claims arising from the lease after actual completion; this includes claims which are unenforceable against a buyer for want of registration.
(f) The seller takes no responsibility for what rent is lawfully recoverable, nor for whether or how any legislation affects the lease.
(g) If the let land is not wholly within the property, the seller may apportion the rent.

## 4. TITLE AND TRANSFER

### 4.1 Proof of title

4.1.1 Without cost to the buyer, the seller is to provide the buyer with proof of the title to the property and of his ability to transfer it, or to procure its transfer.

4.1.2 Where the property has a registered title the proof is to include official copies of the items referred to in rules 134(1)(a) and (b) and 135(1)(a) of the Land Registration Rules 2003, so far as they are not to be discharged or overridden at or before completion.

4.1.3 Where the property has an unregistered title, the proof is to include:
(a) an abstract of title or an epitome of title with photocopies of the documents, and
(b) production of every document or an abstract, epitome or copy of it with an original marking by a conveyancer either against the original or an examined abstract or an examined copy.

### 4.2 Requisitions

4.2.1 The buyer may not raise requisitions:
(a) on any title shown by the seller before the contract was made
(b) in relation to the matters covered by condition 3.1.2.

4.2.2 Notwithstanding condition 4.2.1, the buyer may, within six working days of a matter coming to his attention after the contract was made, raise written requisitions on that matter. In that event, steps 3 and 4 in condition 4.3.1 apply.

4.2.3 On the expiry of the relevant time limit under condition 4.2.2 or condition 4.3.1, the buyer loses his right to raise requisitions or to make observations.

### 4.3 Timetable

4.3.1 Subject to condition 4.2 and to the extent that the seller did not take the steps described in condition 4.1.1 before the contract was made, the following are the steps for deducing and investigating the title to the property to be taken within the following time limits:

| Step | | Time Limit |
|---|---|---|
| 1. | The seller is to comply with condition 4.1.1 | Immediately after making the contract |
| 2. | The buyer may raise written requisitions | Six working days after either the date of the contract or the date of delivery of the seller's evidence of title on which the requisitions are raised, whichever is the later |
| 3. | The seller is to reply in writing to any requisitions raised | Four working days after receiving the requisitions |
| 4. | The buyer may make written observations on the seller's replies | Three working days after receiving the replies |

The time limit on the buyer's right to raise requisitions applies even where the seller supplies incomplete evidence of his title, but the buyer may, within six working days from delivery of any further evidence, raise further requisitions resulting from that evidence.

4.3.2 The parties are to take the following steps to prepare and agree the transfer of the property within the following time limits:

| Step | | Time Limit |
|---|---|---|
| A. | The buyer is to send the seller a draft transfer | At least twelve working days before completion date |
| B. | The seller is to approve or revise that draft and either return it or retain it for use as the actual transfer | Four working days after delivery of the draft transfer |
| C. | If the draft is returned the buyer is to send an engrossment to the seller | At least five working days before completion date |

4.3.3 Periods of time under conditions 4.3.1 and 4.3.2 may run concurrently.

4.3.4 If the period between the date of the contract and completion date is less than 15 working days, the time limits in conditions 4.2.2, 4.3.1 and 4.3.2 are to be reduced by the same proportion as that period bears to the period of 15 working days. Fractions of a working day are to be rounded down except that the time limit to perform any step is not to be less than one working day.

### 4.4 Defining the property

The seller need not:
(a) prove the exact boundaries of the property
(b) prove who owns fences, ditches, hedges or walls
(c) separately identify parts of the property with different titles further than he may be able to do from information in his possession.

### 4.5 Rents and rentcharges

The fact that a rent or rentcharge, whether payable or receivable by the owner of the property, has been, or will on completion be, informally apportioned is not to be regarded as a defect in title.

### 4.6 Transfer

4.6.1 The buyer does not prejudice his right to raise requisitions, or to require replies to any raised, by taking any steps in relation to preparing or agreeing the transfer.

4.6.2 Subject to condition 4.6.3, the seller is to transfer the property with full title guarantee.

4.6.3 The transfer is to have effect as if the disposition is expressly made subject to all matters covered by condition 3.1.2 and, if the property is leasehold, is to contain a statement that the covenants set out in section 4 of the Law of Property (Miscellaneous Provisions) Act 1994 will not extend to any breach of the tenant's covenants in the lease relating to the physical state of the property.

4.6.4 If after completion the seller will remain bound by any obligation affecting the property which was disclosed to the buyer before the contract was made, but the law does not imply any covenant by the buyer to indemnify the seller against liability for future breaches of it:
(a) the buyer is to covenant in the transfer to indemnify the seller against liability for any future breach of the obligation and to perform it from then on, and
(b) if required by the seller, the buyer is to execute and deliver to the seller on completion a duplicate transfer prepared by the buyer.

4.6.5 The seller is to arrange at his expense that, in relation to every document of title which the buyer does not receive on completion, the buyer is to have the benefit of:
(a) a written acknowledgement of his right to its production, and
(b) a written undertaking for its safe custody (except while it is held by a mortgagee or by someone in a fiduciary capacity).

4.7 **Membership of company**
Where the seller is, or is required to be, a member of a company that has an interest in the property or has management responsibilities for the property or the surrounding areas, the seller is, without cost to the buyer, to provide such documents on completion as will enable the buyer to become a member of that company.

**5. RISK, INSURANCE AND OCCUPATION PENDING COMPLETION**

5.1.1 The property is at the risk of the buyer from the date of the contract

5.1.2 The seller is under no obligation to the buyer to insure the property unless:
(a) the contract provides that a policy effected by or for the seller and insuring the property or any part of it against liability for loss or damage is to continue in force, or
(b) the property or any part of it is let on terms under which the seller (whether as landlord or as tenant) is obliged to insure against loss or damage.

5.1.3 If the seller is obliged to insure the property under condition 5.1.2, the seller is to:
(a) do everything necessary to maintain the policy
(b) permit the buyer to inspect the policy or evidence of its terms
(c) if before completion the property suffers loss or damage:
(i) pay to the buyer on completion the amount of the policy monies which the seller has received, so far as not applied in repairing or reinstating the property, and
(ii) if no final payment has then been received, assign to the buyer, at the buyer's expense, all rights to claim under the policy in such form as the buyer reasonably requires and pending execution of the assignment hold any policy monies received in trust for the buyer
(d) cancel the policy on completion.

5.1.4 Where the property is leasehold and the property, or any building containing it, is insured by a reversioner or other third party, the seller is to use reasonable efforts to ensure that the insurance is maintained until completion and if, before completion, the property or building suffers loss or damage the seller is to assign to the buyer on completion, at the buyer's expense, such rights as the seller may have in the policy monies, in such form as the buyer reasonably requires.

5.1.5 If payment under a policy effected by or for the buyer is reduced, because the property is covered against loss or damage by an insurance policy effected by or on behalf of the seller, then, unless the seller is obliged to insure the property under condition 5.1.2, the purchase price is to be abated by the amount of that reduction.

5.1.6 Section 47 of the Law of Property Act 1925 does not apply.

5.2 **Occupation by buyer**

5.2.1 If the buyer is not already lawfully in the property, and the seller agrees to let him into occupation, the buyer occupies on the following terms.

5.2.2 The buyer is a licensee and not a tenant. The terms of the licence are that the buyer:
(a) cannot transfer it
(b) may permit members of his household to occupy the property
(c) is to pay or indemnify the seller against all outgoings and other expenses in respect of the property
(d) is to pay the seller a fee calculated at the contract rate on a sum equal to the purchase price (less any deposit paid) for the period of the licence
(e) is entitled to any rents and profits from any part of the property which he does not occupy
(f) is to keep the property in as good a state of repair as it was in when he went into occupation (except for fair wear and tear) and is not to alter it
(g) if the property is leasehold, is not to do anything which puts the seller in breach of his obligations in the lease, and
(h) is to quit the property when the licence ends.

5.2.3 The buyer is not in occupation for the purposes of this condition if he merely exercises rights of access given solely to do work agreed by the seller.

5.2.4 The buyer's licence ends on the earliest of: completion date, rescission of the contract or when five working days' notice given by one party to the other takes effect.

5.2.5 If the buyer is in occupation of the property after his licence has come to an end and the contract is subsequently completed he is to pay the seller compensation for his continued occupation calculated at the same rate as the fee mentioned in condition 5.2.2(d).

5.2.6 The buyer's right to raise requisitions is unaffected.

**6. COMPLETION**

6.1 **Date**

6.1.1 Completion date is twenty working days after the date of the contract but time is not of the essence of the contract unless a notice to complete has been served.

6.1.2 If the money due on completion is received after 2.00pm, completion is to be treated, for the purposes only of conditions 6.3 and 7.2, as taking place on the next working day as a result of the buyer's default.

6.1.3 Condition 6.1.2 does not apply and the seller is treated as in default if:
(a) the sale is with vacant possession of the property or any part of it, and
(b) the buyer is ready, able and willing to complete but does not pay the money due on completion until after 2.00pm because the seller has not vacated the property or that part by that time.

6.2 **Arrangements and place**

6.2.1 The buyer's conveyancer and the seller's conveyancer are to co-operate in agreeing arrangements for completing the contract.

6.2.2 Completion is to take place in England and Wales, either at the seller's conveyancer's office or at some other place which the seller reasonably specifies.

6.3 **Apportionments**

6.3.1 On evidence of proper payment being made, income and outgoings of the property are to be apportioned between the parties so far as the change of ownership on completion will affect entitlement to receive or liability to pay them.

6.3.2 If the whole property is sold with vacant possession or the seller exercises his option in condition 7.2.4, apportionment is to be made with effect from the date of actual completion; otherwise, it is to be made from completion date.

6.3.3 In apportioning any sum, it is to be assumed that the seller owns the property until the end of the day from which apportionment is made and that the sum accrues from day to day at the rate at which it is payable on that day.

6.3.4 For the purpose of apportioning income and outgoings, it is to be assumed that they accrue at an equal daily rate throughout the year.

6.3.5 When a sum to be apportioned is not known or easily ascertainable at completion, a provisional apportionment is to be made according to the best estimate available. As soon as the amount is known, a final apportionment is to be made and notified to the other party. Any resulting balance is to be paid no more than ten working days later, and if not then paid the balance is to bear interest at the contract rate from then until payment.

6.3.6 Compensation payable under condition 5.2.5 is not to be apportioned.

6.4 **Amount payable**
The amount payable by the buyer on completion is the purchase price and the contents price (less any deposit already paid to the seller or his agent) adjusted to take account of:
(a) apportionments made under condition 6.3
(b) any compensation to be paid or allowed under condition 7.2
(c) any sum payable under condition 5.1.3.

6.5 **Title deeds**

6.5.1 As soon as the buyer has complied with all his obligations under this contract on completion the seller must hand over the documents of title.

6.5.2 Condition 6.5.1 does not apply to any documents of title relating to land being retained by the seller after completion.

6.6 **Rent receipts**
The buyer is to assume that whoever gave any receipt for a payment of rent or service charge which the seller produces was the person or the agent of the person then entitled to that rent or service charge.

6.7 **Means of payment**
The buyer is to pay the money due on completion by a direct transfer of cleared funds from an account held in the name of a conveyancer at a clearing bank and, if appropriate, an unconditional release of a deposit held by a stakeholder.

6.8 **Notice to complete**

6.8.1 At any time after the time applicable under condition 6.1.2 on completion date, a party who is ready, able and willing to complete may give the other a notice to complete.

6.8.2 The parties are to complete the contract within ten working days of giving a notice to complete, excluding the day on which the notice is given. For this purpose, time is of the essence of the contract.

6.8.3 On receipt of a notice to complete:
(a) if the buyer paid no deposit, he is forthwith to pay a deposit of 10 per cent
(b) if the buyer paid a deposit of less than 10 per cent, he is forthwith to pay a further deposit equal to the balance of that 10 per cent.

**7. REMEDIES**

7.1 **Errors and omissions**

7.1.1 If any plan or statement in the contract, or in the negotiations leading to it, is or was misleading or inaccurate due to an error or omission by the seller, the remedies available to the buyer are as follows.
(a) When there is a material difference between the description or value of the property, or of any of the contents included in the contract, as represented and as it is, the buyer is entitled to damages.
(b) An error or omission only entitles the buyer to rescind the contract:
(i) where it results from fraud or recklessness, or
(ii) where he would be obliged, to his prejudice, to accept property differing substantially (in quantity, quality or tenure) from what the error or omission had led him to expect.

7.1.2 If either party rescinds the contract:
(a) unless the rescission is a result of the buyer's breach of contract the deposit is to be repaid to the buyer with accrued interest
(b) the buyer is to return any documents he received from the seller and is to cancel any registration of the contract.

7.2 **Late completion**

7.2.1 If there is default by either or both of the parties in performing their obligations under the contract and completion is delayed, the party whose total period of default is the greater is to pay compensation to the other party.

7.2.2 Compensation is calculated at the contract rate on an amount equal to the purchase price, less (where the buyer is the paying party) any deposit paid, for the period by which the paying party's default exceeds that of the receiving party, or, if shorter, the period between completion date and actual completion.

7.2.3 Any claim for loss resulting from delayed completion is to be reduced by any compensation paid under this contract.

7.2.4 Where the buyer holds the property as tenant of the seller and completion is delayed, the seller may give notice to the buyer, before the date of actual completion, that he intends to take the net income from the property until completion. If he does so, he cannot claim compensation under condition 7.2.1 as well.

7.3 **After completion**
Completion does not cancel liability to perform any outstanding obligation under this contract.

7.4 **Buyer's failure to comply with notice to complete**

7.4.1 If the buyer fails to complete in accordance with a notice to complete, the following terms apply.

7.4.2 The seller may rescind the contract, and if he does so:
(a) he may:
(i) forfeit and keep any deposit and accrued interest
(ii) resell the property and any contents included in the contract
(iii) claim damages
(b) the buyer is to return any documents he received from the seller and is to cancel any registration of the contract.

7.4.3 The seller retains his other rights and remedies.

7.5 **Seller's failure to comply with notice to complete**

7.5.1 If the seller fails to complete in accordance with a notice to complete, the following terms apply.

7.5.2 The buyer may rescind the contract, and if he does so:
(a) the deposit is to be repaid to the buyer with accrued interest
(b) the buyer is to return any documents he received from the seller and is, at the seller's expense, to cancel any registration of the contract.

7.5.3 The buyer retains his other rights and remedies.

**8. LEASEHOLD PROPERTY**

8.1 **Existing leases**

8.1.1 The following provisions apply to a sale of leasehold land.

8.1.2 The seller having provided the buyer with copies of the documents embodying the lease terms, the buyer is treated as entering into the contract knowing and fully accepting those terms.

8.2 **New leases**

8.2.1 The following provisions apply to a contract to grant a new lease.

8.2.2 The conditions apply so that:
'seller' means the proposed landlord
'buyer' means the proposed tenant
'purchase price' means the premium to be paid on the grant of a lease.

8.2.3 The lease is to be in the form of the draft attached to the contract.

8.2.4 If the term of the new lease will exceed seven years, the seller is to deduce a title which will enable the buyer to register the lease at the Land Registry with an absolute title.

8.2.5 The seller is to engross the lease and a counterpart of it and is to send the counterpart to the buyer at least five working days before completion date.

8.2.6 The buyer is to execute the counterpart and deliver it to the seller on completion.

8.3 **Consent**

8.3.1 (a) The following provisions apply if a consent to let, assign or sub-let is required to complete the contract
(b) In this condition 'consent' means consent in the form which satisfies the requirement to obtain it.

8.3.2 (a) The seller is to apply for the consent at his expense, and to use all reasonable efforts to obtain it
(b) The buyer is to provide all information and references reasonably required.

8.3.3 Unless he is in breach of his obligation under condition 8.3.2, either party may rescind the contract by notice to the other party if three working days before completion date (or before a later date on which the parties have agreed to complete the contract):
(a) the consent has not been given, or
(b) the consent has been given subject to a condition to which a party reasonably objects. In that case, neither party is to be treated as in breach of contract and condition 7.1.2 applies.

**9. CONTENTS**

9.1 The following provisions apply to any contents which are included in the contract, whether or not a separate price is to be paid for them.

9.2 The contract takes effect as a contract for sale of goods.

9.3 The buyer takes the contents in the physical state they are in at the date of the contract.

9.4 Ownership of the contents passes to the buyer on actual completion.

## SPECIAL CONDITIONS

1.  (a) This contract incorporates the Standard Conditions of Sale (Fifth Edition – 2018 revision).
    (b) The terms used in this contract have the same meaning when used in the Conditions.
2.  Subject to the terms of this contract and to the Standard Conditions of Sale, the seller is to transfer the property with either full title guarantee or limited title guarantee, as specified on the front page.
3.  (a) The sale includes those contents which are indicated on the attached list as included in the sale and the buyer is to pay the contents price for them.
    (b) The sale excludes those fixtures which are at the property and are indicated on the attached list as excluded from the sale.
4.  The property is sold with vacant possession.
(or)
4.  ~~The property is sold subject to the following leases or tenancies:~~
5.  Conditions 6.1.2 & 6.1.3 shall take effect as if the time specified in them were [        ] pm rather than [        ] pm.
6.  **Representations**
    Neither party can rely on any representation made by the other, unless made in writing by the other or his conveyancer, but this does not exclude liability for fraud or recklessness.
7.  **Occupier's consent**
    Each occupier identified below agrees with the seller and the buyer, in consideration of their entering into this contract, that the occupier concurs in the sale of the property on the terms of this contract, undertakes to vacate the property on or before the completion date and releases the property and any included fixtures and contents from any right or interest that the occupier may have.
    **Note:** this condition does not apply to occupiers under leases or tenancies subject to which the property is sold.

Names(s) and signature(s) of occupier(s) (if any): ⑤
Name
Signature

Notices may be sent to:
**Seller's conveyancer's name:**

   E-mail address:*

**Buyer's conveyancer's name:**

   E-mail address:*

*Adding an e-mail address authorises service by e-mail see condition 1.3.3(b).


# COMMENTARY

❶ There are incumbrances that affect the title. Inserting 'None' into this field could result in a claim being brought against the firm for misrepresentation. The seller's solicitor must refer to any covenants that will burden the property (as they will run with the property) and therefore burden the future owners.

❷ Although the client has advised that they want completion to be on a specific date, it is not possible to include this at the initial stages of the transaction. The candidate should not make any commitments to the client that this date will be achievable.

❸ The contract rate should either be the Law Society's rate (which is 4% above Barclays Bank base rate) from time to time in force, or another bank (usually the seller's solicitors' bank), for example 4% above the base rate of Barclays Bank.

❹ The contract is a legally binding document. As such, if the amount is incorrect (here the candidate has omitted £1,500 as agreed for the sofa) and there is a breach of contract, the client might be unable to recover the correct amount of purchase monies due to this error. When drafting contracts, it is imperative to be precise and utilise the documents provided to ensure the contract is correct.

5. If the daughter does not sign the contract as an occupier, there is a risk that she could potentially claim a beneficial interest in the property that could override the new owners, and she might refuse to vacate the property. If this were to happen, it could result in a claim against the solicitors' firm if there was any misrepresentation (ie if this information was withheld when asked) or negligence (ignored).

## Does this answer meet the threshold?

It is unlikely that this contract would meet the threshold standard for the SQE2 legal drafting assessment. The additional contents (fittings) have not been included. This could result in the buyer not purchasing the items that they expected to. It also leaves the buyers vulnerable to a potential overriding interest claim by the seller's daughter. When assessed against the SQE2 legal drafting assessment criteria, this answer is not precise or concise, there are legal inaccuracies and potential professional conduct issues could arise.

Below is another example of how a different part of the specification could be assessed in the context of legal drafting on SQE2. As with question 1, you might wish to view pages 2 and 3 of the Standard Conditions of Sale form in Attachment 2 (listing the conditions) in digital format at www.lawsociety.org.uk/topics/property/standard-conditions-of-sale, for easier legibility.

## ■ QUESTION 2

### Email to candidate

**From:** Partner
**Sent:** 3 November 202#
**To:** Candidate
**Subject:** Purchase of 67 Acacia Avenue

I am acting on behalf of siblings Mr Vikesh Khatri and Miss Anita Khatri who are purchasing 67 Acacia Avenue, a semi-detached, freehold property with tenants in situ. The seller is a company called FS Housing Corporation, who currently rents the property to Mr Samuel Okeke under an assured shorthold tenancy agreement (AST) which is not set to expire until 26 July 202# next year (1 year in total).

The clients are purchasing the property as an investment with inheritance monies from their deceased uncle.

They intend to remain in their current properties and will be continuing with Mr Okeke's AST.

They have chosen to hold the property as tenants in common in equal shares.

Exchange of contracts has taken place, and a completion date of 14 November has been agreed between the parties.

**I would be grateful if you could read into the enclosed office copy entries and contract (Attachments 1 and 2) with a view to drafting the transfer (Attachment 3) in readiness for completion.**

Thanks

Partner

**Attachment 1**

Contains public sector information licensed under the Open Government Licence v3.0.

| Official copy of register of title | Title number C896457 | Edition date 14.03.202# |
| --- | --- | --- |

- This official copy shows the entries in the register of title on 29.4.202# at 17:53:31.
- This date must be quoted as the "search from date" in any official search application based on this copy.
- The date at the beginning of an entry is the date on which the entry was made in the register.
- Issued on (29th April 202#).
- Under s. 67 of the Land Registration Act 2002, this copy is admissible in evidence to the same extent as the original.
- For more information about the register of title see Land Registry website www.landregistry.gov.uk or Land Registry Guide 1 – *A guide to the information we keep and how you can obtain it.*
- This title is dealt with by the Land Registry Colford Office.

## A: Property Register
**This register describes the land and estate comprised in the Title.**

South Midlands          :          Wolvervale

1. (29th April 202#) The freehold land shown edged with red on the plan of the above title filed at the registry and being known as 67 Acacia Avenue, Wolvervale, W77 1ED.

## B: Proprietorship Register
**This register specifies the class of title and identifies the owner. It contains any entries that affect the right of disposal.**

**Title Absolute**
1. (29th April 202#) PROPRIETOR(s): FS Housing Corporation whose registered office is 192 Lower Howsell Road, Branfort, B23 6AE.

2. (29th April 202#) The price stated to have been paid on 20th April 202# was £350,000.

3. (29th April 202#) The Transfer to the proprietor contains a covenant to observe and perform the covenants referred to in the Charges Register and of an indemnity in respect thereof.

## C: Charges Register
**This register contains any charges and other matters that affect the land**

1. (21st June 1995) By a Transfer dated 3rd June 1995 made between Malcolm Hughes (1) and Veronica Stott (2) contains restrictive covenants.

Note: Copy transfer filed.

**END OF REGISTER**

**Attachment 2**

# CONTRACT

**Incorporating the
Standard Conditions
of Sale (Fifth Edition –
2018 revision)
© The Law Society**

┌─────── **For Conveyancer's use only** ───────┐

Buyer's conveyancer: _____

Seller's conveyancer: _____

Law Society Formula [A/B/C / Personal Exchange]

This information does not form part of the

Contract

└─────────────────────────────────────────┘

| | |
|---|---|
| **Date** | : 31st October 202# |
| **Seller** | : FS Housing Corporation whose registered office is at 192 Lower Howsell Road, Branfort, B23 6AE. |
| **Buyer** | : Vikesh Khatri of 13 Ferny Hill Lane, Halsall Green, Branfort, B12 9WD and Anita Khatri of 92 Hadfield Road, Crawlerton, Branfort, B9 5LA. |
| **Property (freehold/~~leasehold~~)** | : 67 Acacia Avenue, Wolvervale, W77 1ED. |
| **Title number/~~root of title~~** | : C896457 |
| **Specified incumbrances** | : The covenants contained in entry 1 of the charges register of the title. |
| **Title guarantee (full/~~limited~~)** | : Full |
| **Completion date** | : 14th November 202# |
| **Contract rate** | : The Law Society's interest rate from time to time in force. |
| **Purchase price** | : £357,500 |
| **Deposit** | : £35,750 |
| **Contents price (if separate)** | : |
| **Balance** | : £321,750 |

The seller will sell and the buyer will buy the property for the purchase price.

| **WARNING** | **Signed** |
|---|---|
| This is a formal document, designed to create legal rights and legal obligations. Take advice before using it. | |
| | Seller/Buyer |

# STANDARD CONDITIONS OF SALE (FIFTH EDITION – 2018 REVISION)
## (NATIONAL CONDITIONS OF SALE 25TH EDITION, LAW SOCIETY'S CONDITIONS OF SALE 2011)

## GENERAL

### Definitions
1 In these conditions:
(a) 'accrued interest' means:
  (i) if money has been placed on deposit or in a building society share account, the interest actually earned
  (ii) otherwise, the interest which might reasonably have been earned by depositing the money at interest on seven days' notice of withdrawal with a clearing bank less, in either case, any proper charges for handling the money
(b) 'clearing bank' means a bank admitted by the Bank of England as a direct participant in its CHAPS system
(c) 'completion date' has the meaning given in condition 6.1.1
(d) 'contents price' means any separate amount payable for contents included in the contract
(e) 'contract rate' means the Law Society's interest rate from time to time in force
(f) 'conveyancer' means a solicitor, barrister, duly certified notary public, licensed conveyancer or recognised body under sections 9 or 23 of the Administration of Justice Act 1985
(g) 'lease' includes sub-lease, tenancy and agreement for a lease or sub-lease
(h) 'mortgage' means a mortgage or charge securing the repayment of money
(i) 'notice to complete' means a notice requiring completion of the contract in accordance with condition 6.8
(j) 'public requirement' means any notice, order or proposal given or made (whether before or after the date of the contract) by a body acting on statutory authority
(k) 'requisition' includes objection
(l) 'transfer' includes conveyance and assignment
(m) 'working day' means any day from Monday to Friday (inclusive) which is not Christmas Day, Good Friday or a statutory Bank Holiday.
2 In these conditions the terms 'absolute title' and 'official copies' have the special meanings given to them by the Land Registration Act 2002.
3 A party is ready, able and willing to complete:
(a) if he could be, but for the default of the other party, and
(b) in the case of the seller, even though the property remains subject to a mortgage, if the amount to be paid on completion enables the property to be transferred freed of all mortgages (except any to which the sale is expressly subject).
4 These conditions apply except as varied or excluded by the contract.

### Joint parties
If there is more than one seller or more than one buyer, the obligations which they undertake can be enforced against them all jointly or against each individually.

### Notices and documents
1 A notice required or authorised by the contract must be in writing.
2 Giving a notice or delivering a document to a party's conveyancer has the same effect as giving or delivering it to that party.
3 Where delivery of the original document is not essential, a notice or document is validly given or sent if it is sent:
(a) by fax, or
(b) by e-mail to an e-mail address for the intended recipient given in the contract
4 Subject to conditions 1.3.5 to 1.3.7, a notice is given and a document is delivered when it is received.
5 (a) A notice or document sent through a document exchange is received when it is available for collection.
(b) A notice or document which is received after 4.00pm on a working day, or on a day which is not a working day, is to be treated as having been received on the next working day.
(c) An automated response to a notice or document sent by e-mail that the intended recipient is out of the office is to be treated as proof that the notice or document was not received.
6 Condition 1.3.7 applies unless there is proof:
(a) that a notice or document has not been received, or
(b) of when it was received.
7 A notice or document sent by the following means is treated as having been received as follows:

| | | |
|---|---|---|
| (a) by first-class post: | before 4.00pm on the second working day after posting | |
| (b) by second-class post: | before 4.00pm on the third working day after posting | |
| (c) through a document exchange: | before 4.00pm on the first working day after the day on which it would normally be available for collection by the addressee | |
| (d) by fax: | one hour after despatch | |
| (e) by e-mail: | before 4.00pm on the first working day after despatch. | |

### VAT
1 The purchase price and the contents price are inclusive of any value added tax.
2 All other sums made payable by the contract are exclusive of any value added tax and where a supply is made which is chargeable to value added tax, the recipient of the supply is to pay the supplier (in addition to any other amounts payable under the contract) a sum equal to the value added tax chargeable on that supply.

### Assignment and sub-sales
1 The buyer is not entitled to transfer the benefit of the contract
2 The seller cannot be required to transfer the property in parts or to any person other than the buyer.

### Third party rights
Unless otherwise expressly stated nothing in this contract will create rights pursuant to the Contracts (Rights of Third Parties) Act 1999 in favour of anyone other than the parties to the contract.

## FORMATION

### Date
.1 If the parties intend to make a contract by exchanging duplicate copies by post or through a document exchange, the contract is made when the last copy is posted or deposited at the document exchange.
.2 If the parties' conveyancers agree to treat exchange as taking place before duplicate copies are actually exchanged, the contract is made as so agreed.

### Deposit
.1 The buyer is to pay or send a deposit of 10 per cent of the purchase price no later than the date of the contract.
.2 If a cheque tendered in payment of all or part of the deposit is dishonoured when first presented, the seller may, within seven working days of being notified that the cheque has been dishonoured, give notice to the buyer that the contract is discharged by the buyer's breach.
.3 Conditions 2.2.4 to 2.2.6 do not apply on a sale by auction.
.4 The deposit is to be paid:
(a) by electronic means from an account held in the name of a conveyancer at a clearing bank to an account in the name of the seller's conveyancer or (in a case where condition 2.2.5 applies) a conveyancer nominated by him and maintained at a clearing bank or
(b) to the seller's conveyancer or (in a case where condition 2.2.5 applies) a conveyancer nominated by him by cheque drawn on a solicitor's or licensed conveyancer's client account
.5 If before completion date the seller agrees to buy another property in England and Wales for his residence, he may use all or any part of the deposit as a deposit in that transaction to be held on terms to the same effect as this condition and condition 2.2.6.
.6 Any deposit or part of a deposit not being used in accordance with condition 2.2.5 is to be held by the seller's conveyancer as stakeholder on terms that on completion it is paid to the seller with accrued interest.

### Auctions
.1 On a sale by auction the following conditions apply to the property and, if it is sold in lots, to each lot.
.2 The sale is subject to a reserve price.
.3 The seller, or a person on his behalf, may bid up to the reserve price.
.4 The auctioneer may refuse any bid.

2.3.5 If there is a dispute about a bid, the auctioneer may resolve the dispute or restart the auction at the last undisputed bid.
2.3.6 The deposit is to be paid to the auctioneer as agent for the seller.

## 3. MATTERS AFFECTING THE PROPERTY

### 3.1 Freedom from incumbrances
3.1.1 The seller is selling the property free from incumbrances, other than those mentioned in condition 3.1.2.
3.1.2 The incumbrances subject to which the property is sold are:
(a) those specified in the contract
(b) those discoverable by inspection of the property before the date of the contract.
(c) those the seller does not and could not reasonably know about
(d) those, other than mortgages, which the buyer knows about
(e) entries made before the date of the contract in any public register except those maintained by the Land Registry or its Land Charges Department or by Companies House
(f) public requirements.
3.1.3 After the contract is made, the seller is to give the buyer written details without delay of any new public requirement and of anything in writing which he learns about concerning a matter covered by condition 3.1.2.
3.1.4 The buyer is to bear the cost of complying with any outstanding public requirement and is to indemnify the seller against any liability resulting from a public requirement.

### 3.2 Physical state
3.2.1 The buyer accepts the property in the physical state it is in at the date of the contract unless the seller is building or converting it.
3.2.2 A leasehold property is sold subject to any subsisting breach of a condition or tenant's obligation relating to the physical state of the property which renders the lease liable to forfeiture.
3.2.3 A sub-lease is granted subject to any subsisting breach of a condition or tenant's obligation relating to the physical state of the property which renders the seller's own lease liable to forfeiture.

### 3.3 Leases affecting the property
3.3.1 The following provisions apply if any part of the property is sold subject to a lease.
3.3.2 (a) The seller having provided the buyer with full details of each lease or copies of the documents embodying the lease terms, the buyer is treated as entering into the contract knowing and fully accepting those terms.
(b) The seller is to inform the buyer without delay if the lease ends or if the seller learns of any application by the tenant in connection with the lease; the seller is then to act as the buyer reasonably directs, and the buyer is to indemnify him against all consequent loss and expense.
(c) Except with the buyer's consent, the seller is not to agree to any proposal to change the lease terms nor to take any step to end the lease.
(d) The seller is to inform the buyer without delay of any change to the lease terms which may be proposed or agreed.
(e) The buyer is to indemnify the seller against all claims arising from the lease after actual completion; this includes claims which are unenforceable against a buyer for want of registration.
(f) The seller takes no responsibility for what rent is lawfully recoverable, nor for whether or how any legislation affects the lease.
(g) If the let land is not wholly within the property, the seller may apportion the rent.

## 4. TITLE AND TRANSFER

### 4.1 Proof of title
4.1.1 Without cost to the buyer, the seller is to provide the buyer with proof of the title to the property and of his ability to transfer it, or to procure its transfer.
4.1.2 Where the property has a registered title the proof is to include official copies of the items referred to in rules 134(1)(a) and (b) and 135(1)(a) of the Land Registration Rules 2003, so far as they are not to be discharged or overridden at or before completion.
4.1.3 Where the property has an unregistered title, the proof is to include:
(a) an abstract of title or an epitome of title with photocopies of the documents, and
(b) production of every document or an abstract, epitome or copy of it with an original marking by a conveyancer either against the original or an examined abstract or an examined copy.

### 4.2 Requisitions
4.2.1 The buyer may not raise requisitions:
(a) on any title shown by the seller before the contract was made
(b) in relation to the matters covered by condition 3.1.2.
4.2.2 Notwithstanding condition 4.2.1, the buyer may, within six working days of a matter coming to his attention after the contract was made, raise written requisitions on that matter. In that event, steps 3 and 4 in condition 4.3.1 apply.
4.2.3 On the expiry of the relevant time limit under condition 4.2.2 or condition 4.3.1, the buyer loses his right to raise requisitions or to make observations.

### 4.3 Timetable
4.3.1 Subject to condition 4.2 and to the extent that the seller did not take the steps described in condition 4.1.1 before the contract was made, the following are the steps for deducing and investigating the title to the property to be taken within the following time limits:

| Step | | Time Limit |
|---|---|---|
| 1. | The seller is to comply with condition 4.1.1 | Immediately after making the contract |
| 2. | The buyer may raise written requisitions | Six working days after either the date of the contract or the date of delivery of the seller's evidence of title on which the requisitions are raised, whichever is the later |
| 3. | The seller is to reply in writing to any requisitions raised | Four working days after receiving the requisitions |
| 4. | The buyer may make written observations on the seller's replies | Three working days after receiving the replies |

The time limit on the buyer's right to raise requisitions applies even where the seller supplies incomplete evidence of his title, but the buyer may, within six working days from delivery of any further evidence, raise further requisitions resulting from that evidence.
4.3.2 The parties are to take the following steps to prepare and agree the transfer of the property within the following time limits:

| Step | | Time Limit |
|---|---|---|
| A. | The buyer is to send the seller a draft transfer | At least twelve working days before completion date |
| B. | The seller is to approve or revise that draft and either return it or retain it for use as the actual transfer | Four working days after delivery of the draft transfer |
| C. | If the draft is returned the buyer is to send an engrossment to the seller | At least five working days before completion date |

4.3.3 Periods of time under conditions 4.3.1 and 4.3.2 may run concurrently.
4.3.4 If the period between the date of the contract and completion date is less than 15 working days, the time limits in conditions 4.2.2, 4.3.1 and 4.3.2 are to be reduced by the same proportion as that period bears to the period of 15 working days. Fractions of a working day are to be rounded down except that the time limit to perform any step is not to be less than one working day.

### 4.4 Defining the property
The seller need not:
(a) prove the exact boundaries of the property
(b) prove who owns fences, ditches, hedges or walls
(c) separately identify parts of the property with different titles further than he may be able to do from information in his possession.

### 4.5 Rents and rentcharges
The fact that a rent or rentcharge, whether payable or receivable by the owner of the property, has been, or will on completion be, informally apportioned is not to be regarded as a defect in title.

### 4.6 Transfer
4.6.1 The buyer does not prejudice his right to raise requisitions, or to require replies to any raised, by taking any steps in relation to preparing or agreeing the transfer.
4.6.2 Subject to condition 4.6.3, the seller is to transfer the property with full title guarantee.

4.6.3 The transfer is to have effect as if the disposition is expressly made subject to all matters covered by condition 3.1.2 and, if the property is leasehold, is to contain a statement that the covenants set out in section 4 of the Law of Property (Miscellaneous Provisions) Act 1994 will not extend to any breach of the tenant's covenants in the lease relating to the physical state of the property.

4.6.4 If after completion the seller will remain bound by any obligation affecting the property which was disclosed to the buyer before the contract was made, but the law does not imply any covenant by the buyer to indemnify the seller against liability for future breaches of it:
(a) the buyer is to covenant in the transfer to indemnify the seller against liability for any future breach of the obligation and to perform it from then on, and
(b) if required by the seller, the buyer is to execute and deliver to the seller on completion a duplicate transfer prepared by the buyer.

4.6.5 The seller is to arrange at his expense that, in relation to every document of title which the buyer does not receive on completion, the buyer is to have the benefit of:
(a) a written acknowledgement of his right to its production, and
(b) a written undertaking for its safe custody (except while it is held by a mortgagee or by someone in a fiduciary capacity).

4.7 **Membership of company**
Where the seller is, or is required to be, a member of a company that has an interest in the property or has management responsibilities for the property or the surrounding areas, the seller is, without cost to the buyer, to provide such documents on completion as will enable the buyer to become a member of that company.

**5. RISK, INSURANCE AND OCCUPATION PENDING COMPLETION**

5.1.1 The property is at the risk of the buyer from the date of the contract

5.1.2 The seller is under no obligation to the buyer to insure the property unless:
(a) the contract provides that a policy effected by or for the seller and insuring the property or any part of it against liability for loss or damage is to continue in force, or
(b) the property or any part of it is let on terms under which the seller (whether as landlord or as tenant) is obliged to insure against loss or damage.

5.1.3 If the seller is obliged to insure the property under condition 5.1.2, the seller is to:
(a) do everything necessary to maintain the policy
(b) permit the buyer to inspect the policy or evidence of its terms
(c) if before completion the property suffers loss or damage:
(i) pay to the buyer on completion the amount of the policy monies which the seller has received, so far as not applied in repairing or reinstating the property, and
(ii) if no final payment has then been received, assign to the buyer, at the buyer's expense, all rights to claim under the policy in such form as the buyer reasonably requires and pending execution of the assignment hold any policy monies received in trust for the buyer
(d) cancel the policy on completion.

5.1.4 Where the property is leasehold and the property, or any building containing it, is insured by a reversioner or other third party, the seller is to use reasonable efforts to ensure that the insurance is maintained until completion and if, before completion, the property or building suffers loss or damage the seller is to assign to the buyer on completion, at the buyer's expense, such rights as the seller may have in the policy monies, in such form as the buyer reasonably requires.

5.1.5 If payment under a policy effected by or for the buyer is reduced, because the property is covered against loss or damage by an insurance policy effected by or on behalf of the seller, then, unless the seller is obliged to insure the property under condition 5.1.2, the purchase price is to be abated by the amount of that reduction.

5.1.6 Section 47 of the Law of Property Act 1925 does not apply.

5.2 **Occupation by buyer**

5.2.1 If the buyer is not already lawfully in the property, and the seller agrees to let him into occupation, the buyer occupies on the following terms.

5.2.2 The buyer is a licensee and not a tenant. The terms of the licence are that the buyer:
(a) cannot transfer it
(b) may permit members of his household to occupy the property
(c) is to pay or indemnify the seller against all outgoings and other expenses in respect of the property
(d) is to pay the seller a fee calculated at the contract rate on a sum equal to the purchase price (less any deposit paid) for the period of the licence
(e) is entitled to any rents and profits from any part of the property which he does not occupy
(f) is to keep the property in as good a state of repair as it was in when he went into occupation (except for fair wear and tear) and is not to alter it
(g) if the property is leasehold, is not to do anything which puts the seller in breach of his obligations in the lease, and
(h) is to quit the property when the licence ends.

5.2.3 The buyer is not in occupation for the purposes of this condition if he merely exercises rights of access given solely to do work agreed by the seller.

5.2.4 The buyer's licence ends on the earliest of: completion date, rescission of the contract or when five working days' notice given by one party to the other takes effect.

5.2.5 If the buyer is in occupation of the property after his licence has come to an end and the contract is subsequently completed he is to pay the seller compensation for his continued occupation calculated at the same rate as the fee mentioned in condition 5.2.2(d).

5.2.6 The buyer's right to raise requisitions is unaffected.

**6. COMPLETION**

6.1 **Date**

6.1.1 Completion date is twenty working days after the date of the contract but time is not of the essence of the contract unless a notice to complete has been served.

6.1.2 If the money due on completion is received after 2.00pm, completion is to be treated, for the purposes only of conditions 6.3 and 7.2, as taking place on the next working day as a result of the buyer's default.

6.1.3 Condition 6.1.2 does not apply and the seller is treated as in default if:
(a) the sale is with vacant possession of the property or any part of it, and
(b) the buyer is ready, able and willing to complete but does not pay the money due on completion until after 2.00pm because the seller has not vacated the property or that part by that time.

6.2 **Arrangements and place**

6.2.1 The buyer's conveyancer and the seller's conveyancer are to co-operate in agreeing arrangements for completing the contract.

6.2.2 Completion is to take place in England and Wales, either at the seller's conveyancer's office or at some other place which the seller reasonably specifies.

6.3 **Apportionments**

6.3.1 On evidence of proper payment being made, income and outgoings of the property are to be apportioned between the parties so far as the change of ownership on completion will affect entitlement to receive or liability to pay them.

6.3.2 If the whole property is sold with vacant possession or the seller exercises his option in condition 7.2.4, apportionment is to be made with effect from the date of actual completion; otherwise, it is to be made from completion date.

6.3.3 In apportioning any sum, it is to be assumed that the seller owns the property until the end of the day from which apportionment is made and that the sum accrues from day to day at the rate at which it is payable on that day.

6.3.4 For the purpose of apportioning income and outgoings, it is to be assumed that they accrue at an equal daily rate throughout the year.

6.3.5 When a sum to be apportioned is not known or easily ascertainable at completion, a provisional apportionment is to be made according to the best estimate available. As soon as the amount is known, a final apportionment is to be made and notified to the other party. Any resulting balance is to be paid no more than ten working days later, and if not then paid the balance is to bear interest at the contract rate from then until payment.

6.3.6 Compensation payable under condition 5.2.5 is not to be apportioned.

6.4 **Amount payable**
The amount payable by the buyer on completion is the purchase price and the contents price (less any deposit already paid to the seller or his agent) adjusted to take account of:
(a) apportionments made under condition 6.3
(b) any compensation to be paid or allowed under condition 7.2
(c) any sum payable under condition 5.1.3.

6.5 **Title deeds**

6.5.1 As soon as the buyer has complied with all his obligations under this contract on completion the seller must hand over the documents of title.

6.5.2 Condition 6.5.1 does not apply to any documents of title relating to land being retained by the seller after completion.

6.6 **Rent receipts**
The buyer is to assume that whoever gave any receipt for a payment of rent or service charge which the seller produces was the person or the agent of the person then entitled to that rent or service charge.

6.7 **Means of payment**
The buyer is to pay the money due on completion by a direct transfer of cleared funds from an account held in the name of a conveyancer at a clearing bank and, if appropriate, an unconditional release of a deposit held by a stakeholder.

6.8 **Notice to complete**

6.8.1 At any time after the time applicable under condition 6.1.2 on completion date, a party who is ready, able and willing to complete may give the other a notice to complete.

6.8.2 The parties are to complete the contract within ten working days of giving a notice to complete, excluding the day on which the notice is given. For this purpose, time is of the essence of the contract.

6.8.3 On receipt of a notice to complete:
(a) if the buyer paid no deposit, he is forthwith to pay a deposit of 10 per cent
(b) if the buyer paid a deposit of less than 10 per cent, he is forthwith to pay a further deposit equal to the balance of that 10 per cent.

**7. REMEDIES**

7.1 **Errors and omissions**

7.1.1 If any plan or statement in the contract, or in the negotiations leading to it, is or was misleading or inaccurate due to an error or omission by the seller, the remedies available to the buyer are as follows.
(a) When there is a material difference between the description or value of the property, or of any of the contents included in the contract, as represented and as it is, the buyer is entitled to damages.
(b) An error or omission only entitles the buyer to rescind the contract:
(i) where it results from fraud or recklessness, or
(ii) where he would be obliged, to his prejudice, to accept property differing substantially (in quantity, quality or tenure) from what the error or omission had led him to expect.

7.1.2 If either party rescinds the contract:
(a) unless the rescission is a result of the buyer's breach of contract the deposit is to be repaid to the buyer with accrued interest
(b) the buyer is to return any documents he received from the seller and is to cancel any registration of the contract.

7.2 **Late completion**

7.2.1 If there is default by either or both of the parties in performing their obligations under the contract and completion is delayed, the party whose total period of default is the greater is to pay compensation to the other party.

7.2.2 Compensation is calculated at the contract rate on an amount equal to the purchase price, less (where the buyer is the paying party) any deposit paid, for the period by which the paying party's default exceeds that of the receiving party, or, if shorter, the period between completion date and actual completion.

7.2.3 Any claim for loss resulting from delayed completion is to be reduced by any compensation paid under this contract.

7.2.4 Where the buyer holds the property as tenant of the seller and completion is delayed, the seller may give notice to the buyer, before the date of actual completion, that he intends to take the net income from the property until completion. If he does so, he cannot claim compensation under condition 7.2.1 as well.

7.3 **After completion**
Completion does not cancel liability to perform any outstanding obligation under this contract.

7.4 **Buyer's failure to comply with notice to complete**

7.4.1 If the buyer fails to complete in accordance with a notice to complete, the following terms apply.

7.4.2 The seller may rescind the contract, and if he does so:
(a) he may:
(i) forfeit and keep any deposit and accrued interest
(ii) resell the property and any contents included in the contract
(iii) claim damages
(b) the buyer is to return any documents he received from the seller and is to cancel any registration of the contract.

7.4.3 The seller retains his other rights and remedies.

7.5 **Seller's failure to comply with notice to complete**

7.5.1 If the seller fails to complete in accordance with a notice to complete, the following terms apply.

7.5.2 The buyer may rescind the contract, and if he does so:
(a) the deposit is to be repaid to the buyer with accrued interest
(b) the buyer is to return any documents he received from the seller and is, at the seller's expense, to cancel any registration of the contract.

7.5.3 The buyer retains his other rights and remedies.

**8. LEASEHOLD PROPERTY**

8.1 **Existing leases**

8.1.1 The following provisions apply to a sale of leasehold land.

8.1.2 The seller having provided the buyer with copies of the documents embodying the lease terms, the buyer is treated as entering into the contract knowing and fully accepting those terms.

8.2 **New leases**

8.2.1 The following provisions apply to a contract to grant a new lease.

8.2.2 The conditions apply so that:
'seller' means the proposed landlord
'buyer' means the proposed tenant
'purchase price' means the premium to be paid on the grant of a lease.

8.2.3 The lease is to be in the form of the draft attached to the contract.

8.2.4 If the term of the new lease will exceed seven years, the seller is to deduce a title which will enable the buyer to register the lease at the Land Registry with an absolute title.

8.2.5 The seller is to engross the lease and a counterpart of it and is to send the counterpart to the buyer at least five working days before completion date.

8.2.6 The buyer is to execute the counterpart and deliver it to the seller on completion.

8.3 **Consent**

8.3.1 (a) The following provisions apply if a consent to let, assign or sub-let is required to complete the contract
(b) In this condition 'consent' means consent in the form which satisfies the requirement to obtain it.

8.3.2 (a) The seller is to apply for the consent at his expense, and to use all reasonable efforts to obtain it
(b) The buyer is to provide all information and references reasonably required.

8.3.3 Unless he is in breach of his obligation under condition 8.3.2, either party may rescind the contract by notice to the other party if three working days before completion date (or before a later date on which the parties have agreed to complete the contract):
(a) the consent has not been given, or
(b) the consent has been given subject to a condition to which a party reasonably objects. In that case, neither party is to be treated as in breach of contract and condition 7.1.2 applies.

**9. CONTENTS**

9.1 The following provisions apply to any contents which are included in the contract, whether or not a separate price is to be paid for them.

9.2 The contract takes effect as a contract for sale of goods.

9.3 The buyer takes the contents in the physical state they are in at the date of the contract.

9.4 Ownership of the contents passes to the buyer on actual completion.

## SPECIAL CONDITIONS

1.  (a) This contract incorporates the Standard Conditions of Sale (Fifth Edition – 2018 revision).
    (b) The terms used in this contract have the same meaning when used in the Conditions.
2.  Subject to the terms of this contract and to the Standard Conditions of Sale, the seller is to transfer the property with either full title guarantee or limited title guarantee, as specified on the front page.
3.  (a) The sale includes those contents which are indicated on the attached list as included in the sale and the buyer is to pay the contents price for them.
    (b) The sale excludes those fixtures which are at the property and are indicated on the attached list as excluded from the sale.
4.  ~~The property is sold with vacant possession on completion~~
(or)
4.  The property is sold subject to the following leases or tenancies:
    Assured Shorthold Tenancy Agreement dated 26th July 202# between FS Housing Corporation and Samuel Okeke.
5.  Conditions 6.1.2 & 6.1.3 shall take effect as if the time specified in them were [      ] pm rather than [      ] pm.
6.  **Representations**
    Neither party can rely on any representation made by the other, unless made in writing by the other or his conveyancer, but this does not exclude liability for fraud or recklessness.
7.  **Occupier's consent**
    Each occupier identified below agrees with the seller and the buyer, in consideration of their entering into this contract, that the occupier concurs in the sale of the property on the terms of this contract, undertakes to vacate the property on or before the completion date and releases the property and any included fixtures and contents from any right or interest that the occupier may have.

    **Note:** this condition does not apply to occupiers under leases or tenancies subject to which the property is sold.

Names(s) and signature(s) of occupier(s) (if any):
Name
Signature

Notices may be sent to:
**Seller's conveyancer's name:**
CLM Solicitors

    E-mail address:*

**Buyer's conveyancer's name:**
RD & Co Solicitors

    E-mail address:*

*Adding an e-mail address authorises service by e-mail see condition 1.3.3(b)

**Attachment 3**

# HM Land Registry
Transfer of whole of registered title(s)

# TR1

**Any parts of the form that are not typed should be completed in black ink and in block capitals.**

If you need more room than is provided for in a panel, and your software allows, you can expand any panel in the form. Alternatively use continuation sheet CS and attach it to this form.

For information on how HM Land Registry processes your personal information, see our Personal Information Charter.

| | |
|---|---|
| Leave blank if not yet registered. | 1  Title number(s) of the property: |
| Insert address including postcode (if any) or other description of the property, for example 'land adjoining 2 Acacia Avenue'. | 2  Property: |
| Remember to date this deed with the day of completion, but not before it has been signed and witnessed. | 3  Date: |
| Give full name(s) of **all** the persons transferring the property.<br><br>Complete as appropriate where the transferor is a company.<br><br>Enter the overseas entity ID issued by Companies House for the transferor pursuant to the Economic Crime (Transparency and Enforcement) Act 2022. If the ID is not required, you may instead state 'not required'.<br><br>Further details on overseas entities can be found in practice guide 78: overseas entities. | 4  Transferor:<br><br>*For UK incorporated companies/LLPs*<br>Registered number of company or limited liability partnership including any prefix:<br><br>*For overseas entities*<br>(a)  Territory of incorporation or formation:<br><br>(b)  Overseas entity ID issued by Companies House, including any prefix:<br><br>(c)  Where the entity is a company with a place of business in the United Kingdom, the registered number, if any, issued by Companies House, including any prefix: |

Give full name(s) of **all** the persons to be shown as registered proprietors.

Complete as appropriate where the transferee is a company. Also, for an overseas company, unless an arrangement with HM Land Registry exists, lodge either a certificate in Form 7 in Schedule 3 to the Land Registration Rules 2003 or a certified copy of the constitution in English or Welsh, or other evidence permitted by rule 183 of the Land Registration Rules 2003.

Enter the overseas entity ID issued by Companies House for the transferee pursuant to the Economic Crime (Transparency and Enforcement) Act 2022. If the ID is not required, you may instead state 'not required'.

Further details on overseas entities can be found in practice guide 78: overseas entities.

| 5 | Transferee for entry in the register: |
|---|---|

*For UK incorporated companies/LLPs*
Registered number of company or limited liability partnership including any prefix:

For overseas entities
(a) Territory of incorporation or formation:

(b) Overseas entity ID issued by Companies House, including any prefix:

(c) Where the entity is a company with a place of business in the United Kingdom, the registered number, if any, issued by Companies House, including any prefix:

---

Each transferee may give up to three addresses for service, one of which must be a postal address whether or not in the UK (including the postcode, if any). The others can be any combination of a postal address, a UK DX box number or an email address.

| 6 | Transferee's intended address(es) for service for entry in the register: |
|---|---|

---

| 7 | The transferor transfers the property to the transferee |
|---|---|

---

Place 'X' in the appropriate box. State the currency unit if other than sterling. If none of the boxes apply, insert an appropriate memorandum in panel 11.

| 8 | Consideration |
|---|---|
|  | ☐ The transferor has received from the transferee for the property the following sum (in words and figures): |
|  | ☐ The transfer is not for money or anything that has a monetary value |
|  | ☐ Insert other receipt as appropriate: |

---

Place 'X' in any box that applies.

Add any modifications.

| 9 | The transferor transfers with |
|---|---|
|  | ☐ full title guarantee |
|  | ☐ limited title guarantee |

Where the transferee is more than one person, place 'X' in the appropriate box.

Complete as necessary.

The registrar will enter a Form A restriction in the register *unless*:
- [ ] an 'X' is placed:
- [ ] in the first box, or
- [ ] in the third box and the details of the trust or of the trust instrument show that the transferees are to hold the property on trust for themselves alone as joint tenants, *or*
- [ ] it is clear from completion of a form JO lodged with this application that the transferees are to hold the property on trust for themselves alone as joint tenants.

Please refer to *Joint property ownership* and practice guide *24: private trusts of land* for further guidance. These are both available on the GOV.UK website.

Insert here any required or permitted statement, certificate or application and any agreed covenants, declarations and so on.

The transferor must execute this transfer as a deed using the space opposite. If there is more than one transferor, all must execute. Forms of execution are given in Schedule 9 to the Land Registration Rules 2003. If the transfer contains transferee's covenants or declarations or contains an application by the transferee (such as for a restriction), it must also be executed by the transferee.

---

10    Declaration of trust. The transferee is more than one person and
- [ ] they are to hold the property on trust for themselves as joint tenants
- [ ] they are to hold the property on trust for themselves as tenants in common in equal shares
- [ ] they are to hold the property on trust:

11    Additional provisions

12    Execution

If there is more than one transferee and panel 10 has been completed, each transferee must also execute this transfer to comply with the requirements in section 53(1)(b) of the Law of Property Act 1925 relating to the declaration of a trust of land. Please refer to *Joint property ownership* and practice guide *24: private trusts of land* for further guidance.

Examples of the correct form of execution are set out in practice guide 8: execution of deeds. Execution as a deed usually means that a witness must also sign, and add their name and address.

Remember to date this deed in panel 3.

WARNING
If you dishonestly enter information or make a statement that you know is, or might be, untrue or misleading, and intend by doing so to make a gain for yourself or another person, or to cause loss or the risk of loss to another person, you may commit the offence of fraud under section 1 of the Fraud Act 2006, the maximum penalty for which is 10 years' imprisonment or an unlimited fine, or both.

Failure to complete this form with proper care may result in a loss of protection under the Land Registration Act 2002 if, as a result, a mistake is made in the register.

Under section 66 of the Land Registration Act 2002 most documents (including this form) kept by the registrar relating to an application to the registrar or referred to in the register are open to public inspection and copying. If you believe a document contains prejudicial information, you may apply for that part of the document to be made exempt using Form EX1, under rule 136 of the Land Registration Rules 2003.

© Crown copyright (ref: LR/HO) 08/23

\*   \*   \*

## ■ YOUR TURN

Have a go at answering question 2, remembering the guidance on pages 74–75.
- Refer to the structured approach in the SRA's assessment criteria on page 75.
- Create a list of the most important pieces of information to assist with drafting the transfer.
- Timings are important: you will need to prepare and write your answer in 45 minutes.

| SQE1 Functioning legal knowledge link |
| --- |
| Remember from chapter 5 of *Revise SQE: Property Practice* the importance of ensuring that the transfer is correctly executed as a deed in order to validly convey the legal estate. |

## EVALUATING YOUR ANSWER

When you have attempted question 2, mark it yourself against the SQE2 legal drafting assessment criteria. Do you think your attempt met the threshold standard?

Now compare your attempt with the following key legal points and two sample answers to question 2. A circled number indicates that commentary is provided for this part of the answer. The commentary will explain whether or not the sample is likely to meet the threshold SQE2 standard.

---

### ➡Key legal points: Question 2

- The clients have advised that they wish to hold the property as tenants in common. Therefore, the declaration of trust will need to be correctly recorded in the transfer to allow for a Form A restriction to be added to the title, to prevent the sale of a sole legal owner in the future.
- In relation to additional provisions, an indemnity covenant should be added to a transfer where there is a chain of indemnity, to ensure that should any covenants be breached in the future, liability will remain with the new legal owners.
- If there is no mention of the company's articles of association, executing a transfer on behalf of a company can be done in two ways:
  a) The company acts by two directors or two directors and the company secretary (if they are one and the same).
  b) A single director can sign on behalf of the company, alongside an independent witness.

---

### ■ SAMPLE ANSWER 1 TO QUESTION 2

# HM Land Registry
Transfer of whole of registered title(s)                           # TR1

**Any parts of the form that are not typed should be completed in black ink and in block capitals.**

If you need more room than is provided for in a panel, and your software allows, you can expand any panel in the form. Alternatively use continuation sheet CS and attach it to this form.

For information on how HM Land Registry processes your personal information, see our Personal Information Charter.

| | |
|---|---|
| Leave blank if not yet registered. | 1  Title number(s) of the property:<br>C896457 |
| Insert address including postcode (if any) or other description of the property, for example 'land adjoining 2 Acacia Avenue'. | 2  Property:<br>67 Acacia Avenue, Wolvervale, W77 1ED. |
| Remember to date this deed with the day of completion, but not before it has been signed and witnessed. | 3  Date: ❶ |

| | |
|---|---|
| Give full name(s) of **all** the persons transferring the property.<br><br>Complete as appropriate where the transferor is a company.<br><br>Enter the overseas entity ID issued by Companies House for the transferor pursuant to the Economic Crime (Transparency and Enforcement) Act 2022. If the ID is not required, you may instead state 'not required'.<br><br>Further details on overseas entities can be found in practice guide 78: overseas entities. | 4   Transferor:<br>FS Housing Corporation<br><br>*For UK incorporated companies/LLPs*<br>Registered number of company or limited liability partnership including any prefix:<br><br>*For overseas entities*<br>(a) Territory of incorporation or formation:<br><br>(b) Overseas entity ID issued by Companies House, including any prefix:<br><br>(c) Where the entity is a company with a place of business in the United Kingdom, the registered number, if any, issued by Companies House, including any prefix: |
| Give full name(s) of **all** the persons to be shown as registered proprietors.<br><br>Complete as appropriate where the transferee is a company. Also, for an overseas company, unless an arrangement with HM Land Registry exists, lodge either a certificate in Form 7 in Schedule 3 to the Land Registration Rules 2003 or a certified copy of the constitution in English or Welsh, or other evidence permitted by rule 183 of the Land Registration Rules 2003.<br><br>Enter the overseas entity ID issued by Companies House for the transferee pursuant to the Economic Crime (Transparency and Enforcement) Act 2022. If the ID is not required, you may instead state 'not required'.<br><br>Further details on overseas entities can be found in practice guide 78: overseas entities. | 5   Transferee for entry in the register:<br>Vikesh Khatri and Anita Khatri<br><br>*For UK incorporated companies/LLPs*<br>Registered number of company or limited liability partnership including any prefix:<br><br>*For overseas entities*<br>(a) Territory of incorporation or formation:<br><br>(b) Overseas entity ID issued by Companies House, including any prefix:<br><br>(c) Where the entity is a company with a place of business in the United Kingdom, the registered number, if any, issued by Companies House, including any prefix: |
| Each transferee may give up to three addresses for service, one of which must be a postal address whether or not in the UK (including the postcode, if any). The others can be any combination of a postal address, a UK DX box number or an email address. | 6   Transferee's intended address(es) for service for entry in the register:<br>13 Ferny Hill Lane, Halsall Green, Branfort, B12 9WD.<br>92 Hadfield Road, Crawlerton, Branfort, B9 5LA. ❷ |
| | 7   The transferor transfers the property to the transferee |

| Place 'X' in the appropriate box. State the currency unit if other than sterling. If none of the boxes apply, insert an appropriate memorandum in panel 11. | 8 Consideration<br>☒ The transferor has received from the transferee for the property the following sum (in words and figures):<br><br>Three Hundred and Fifty Seven Thousand and Five Hundred Pounds (£357,500).<br><br>☐ The transfer is not for money or anything that has a monetary value<br>☐ Insert other receipt as appropriate: |
|---|---|
| Place 'X' in any box that applies.<br><br>Add any modifications. | 9 The transferor transfers with<br>☒ full title guarantee<br>☐ limited title guarantee |
| Where the transferee is more than one person, place 'X' in the appropriate box.<br><br>Complete as necessary.<br><br>The registrar will enter a Form A restriction in the register *unless*:<br>☐ an 'X' is placed:<br>☐ in the first box, or<br>☐ in the third box and the details of the trust or of the trust instrument show that the transferees are to hold the property on trust for themselves alone as joint tenants, *or*<br>☐ it is clear from completion of a form JO lodged with this application that the transferees are to hold the property on trust for themselves alone as joint tenants.<br><br>Please refer to *Joint property ownership* and practice guide *24: private trusts of land* for further guidance. These are both available on the GOV.UK website. | 10 Declaration of trust. The transferee is more than one person and<br>☐ they are to hold the property on trust for themselves as joint tenants<br>☒ they are to hold the property on trust for themselves as tenants in common in equal shares ❸<br>☐ they are to hold the property on trust: |
| Insert here any required or permitted statement, certificate or application and any agreed covenants, declarations and so on. | 11 Additional provisions<br><br>The Transferee/s hereby covenant/s with the Transferor/s by way of indemnity only to observe and perform the covenants contained or referred to in the registers of title number C896457 and to indemnify the transferor against any liability incurred for any breach or non-observance of the Covenants occurring after the date of this transfer. ❹ |

The transferor must execute this transfer as a deed using the space opposite. If there is more than one transferor, all must execute. Forms of execution are given in Schedule 9 to the Land Registration Rules 2003. If the transfer contains transferee's covenants or declarations or contains an application by the transferee (such as for a restriction), it must also be executed by the transferee.

If there is more than one transferee and panel 10 has been completed, each transferee must also execute this transfer to comply with the requirements in section 53(1)(b) of the Law of Property Act 1925 relating to the declaration of a trust of land. Please refer to *Joint property ownership* and practice guide *24: private trusts of land* for further guidance.

Examples of the correct form of execution are set out in practice guide 8: execution of deeds. Execution as a deed usually means that a witness must also sign, and add their name and address.

Remember to date this deed in panel 3.

---

**12    Execution**

Executed as a Deed by ⑤

FS Housing Corporation

Acting by

.........................................................................
[signature of director]

Director

.........................................................................
[signature of director/secretary]

Director OR Secretary

Signed as a Deed by

Vikesh Khatri ........................................................

In the presence of

Signature of witness ........................................

Name (in BLOCK CAPITALS) ....................
.........................................................................

Address ...............................................................
.........................................................................

Signed as a Deed by

Anita Khatri .........................................................

In the presence of

Signature of witness ........................................

Name (in BLOCK CAPITALS) .........................
.........................................................................

Address ...............................................................
.........................................................................

---

WARNING
If you dishonestly enter information or make a statement that you know is, or might be, untrue or misleading, and intend by doing so to make a gain for yourself or another person, or to cause loss or the risk of loss to another person, you may commit the offence of fraud under section 1 of the Fraud Act 2006, the maximum penalty for which is 10 years' imprisonment or an unlimited fine, or both.

Failure to complete this form with proper care may result in a loss of protection under the Land Registration Act 2002 if, as a result, a mistake is made in the register.

Under section 66 of the Land Registration Act 2002 most documents (including this form) kept by the registrar relating to an application to the registrar or referred to in the register are open to public inspection and copying. If you believe a document contains prejudicial information, you may apply for that part of the document to be made exempt using Form EX1, under rule 136 of the Land Registration Rules 2003.

## COMMENTARY

**1** A transfer should not be dated until the transaction has been completed. This is because, although a completion date may have been agreed, until completion monies have been transferred there is always a possibility of delayed completion. It is standard practice to provide a copy of the transfer to the client for signing with the words 'DO NOT DATE' in pencil to avoid any problems.

**2** Panel 6 of the transfer is to confirm to the Land Registry where to send any notifications. It is usually the address of the property being purchased if the clients are moving into the property. However, in this instance, the clients are not moving into the property. To avoid any potential problems with the title, such as someone trying to register a charge on the property, the registered address should be where the clients reside to allow for them to be contacted without delay. Up to three addresses can be provided in this panel; from an ethical standpoint, as the candidate is acting for both clients in this instance, both addresses should be inserted here unless they have specific instructions only to provide one address.

**3** As there are going to be two legal owners on the title, it is important to ascertain from the clients how they wish to hold the beneficial title upon completion. The attendance note specifically states that they have chosen to hold the beneficial title as tenants in common, so this box should be checked. This shows the examiner that the candidate is utilising the information provided and drafting a document which is legally comprehensive.

**4** In panel 11, an indemnity covenant should be included because there is an indemnity covenant on the title of the property being purchased. When there are indemnity covenants on the office copy entries, the new owners will need to enter this to protect the sellers from any future breach or non-observance of the covenants on the title (after the date of the transfer). There is standardised wording, and as with this scenario, the buyers will then be required to sign the transfer, agreeing to observe and perform the covenants and indemnify the sellers from any future breaches.

**5** The final panel is extremely important as it must be executed correctly to validly convey the legal estate to the new legal owners. If this is not done, the clients will not be registered as the new legal owners, and this could result in a claim being made against the firm for professional negligence. It is important to note here that as per above, the clients and the sellers will need to sign the transfer because of the indemnity covenant. In addition, as no information is provided on whether the company can affix the company seal (in their articles of association), it will need to be signed by either two directors, or one director and one company secretary. The witness to the signatures should be independent. The correct completion of this panel is a good opportunity to show an examiner that you are able to draft a legally correct transfer.

## Does this answer meet the threshold?

The sample answer above includes all of the components that the transfer requires in order to be a valid deed. It correctly includes address for service to protect the client from any fraudulent attempts to register something against the title, in addition to including a valid execution clause to ensure it is a legal deed. It is, therefore, likely to meet the threshold standard for the SQE2 legal drafting assessment.

Note how each of the assessment criteria for legal drafting are dealt with and, where appropriate, the examiner is directed specifically to the areas of the transfer which deal with those criteria. Remember to show the examiners that you are familiar with the criteria by which you are being assessed.

Now consider the second sample answer to question 2.

## ■ SAMPLE ANSWER 2 TO QUESTION 2

# HM Land Registry
Transfer of whole of registered title(s)

# TR1

**Any parts of the form that are not typed should be completed in black ink and in block capitals.**

If you need more room than is provided for in a panel, and your software allows, you can expand any panel in the form. Alternatively use continuation sheet CS and attach it to this form.

For information on how HM Land Registry processes your personal information, see our Personal Information Charter.

| | |
|---|---|
| Leave blank if not yet registered. | 1  Title number(s) of the property:<br>C896457 |
| Insert address including postcode (if any) or other description of the property, for example 'land adjoining 2 Acacia Avenue'. | 2  Property:<br>67 Acacia Avenue, Wolvervale, W77 1ED. |
| Remember to date this deed with the day of completion, but not before it has been signed and witnessed. | 3  Date: |

Give full name(s) of **all** the persons transferring the property.

Complete as appropriate where the transferor is a company.

Enter the overseas entity ID issued by Companies House for the transferor pursuant to the Economic Crime (Transparency and Enforcement) Act 2022. If the ID is not required, you may instead state 'not required'.

Further details on overseas entities can be found in practice guide 78: overseas entities.

| | |
|---|---|
| 4 | Transferor: |
| | FS Housing Corporation |
| | |
| | *For UK incorporated companies/LLPs* |
| | Registered number of company or limited liability partnership including any prefix: |
| | |
| | *For overseas entities* |
| | (a) Territory of incorporation or formation: |
| | |
| | (b) Overseas entity ID issued by Companies House, including any prefix: |
| | |
| | (c) Where the entity is a company with a place of business in the United Kingdom, the registered number, if any, issued by Companies House, including any prefix: |

Give full name(s) of **all** the persons to be shown as registered proprietors.

Complete as appropriate where the transferee is a company. Also, for an overseas company, unless an arrangement with HM Land Registry exists, lodge either a certificate in Form 7 in Schedule 3 to the Land Registration Rules 2003 or a certified copy of the constitution in English or Welsh, or other evidence permitted by rule 183 of the Land Registration Rules 2003.

Enter the overseas entity ID issued by Companies House for the transferee pursuant to the Economic Crime (Transparency and Enforcement) Act 2022. If the ID is not required, you may instead state 'not required'.

Further details on overseas entities can be found in practice guide 78: overseas entities.

| | |
|---|---|
| 5 | Transferee for entry in the register: |
| | Mr V Khatri and Miss A Khatri ❶ |
| | |
| | *For UK incorporated companies/LLPs* |
| | Registered number of company or limited liability partnership including any prefix: |
| | |
| | *For overseas entities* |
| | (a) Territory of incorporation or formation: |
| | |
| | (b) Overseas entity ID issued by Companies House, including any prefix: |
| | |
| | (c) Where the entity is a company with a place of business in the United Kingdom, the registered number, if any, issued by Companies House, including any prefix: |

Each transferee may give up to three addresses for service, one of which must be a postal address whether or not in the UK (including the postcode, if any). The others can be any combination of a postal address, a UK DX box number or an email address.

| | |
|---|---|
| 6 | Transferee's intended address(es) for service for entry in the register: |
| | 67 Acacia Avenue, Wolvervale, W77 1ED. ❷ |

| | |
|---|---|
| 7 | The transferor transfers the property to the transferee |

Place 'X' in the appropriate box. State the currency unit if other than sterling. If none of the boxes apply, insert an appropriate memorandum in panel 11.

8   Consideration

☒   The transferor has received from the transferee for the property the following sum (in words and figures):

 Three Hundred and Twenty One Thousand, Seven Hundred and Fifty Pounds (£321,750) ❸

☐   The transfer is not for money or anything that has a monetary value

☐   Insert other receipt as appropriate:

Place 'X' in any box that applies.

Add any modifications.

Where the transferee is more than one person, place 'X' in the appropriate box.

Complete as necessary.

The registrar will enter a Form A restriction in the register *unless*:

☐   an 'X' is placed:

☐   in the first box, or

☐   in the third box and the details of the trust or of the trust instrument show that the transferees are to hold the property on trust for themselves alone as joint tenants, *or*

☐   it is clear from completion of a form JO lodged with this application that the transferees are to hold the property on trust for themselves alone as joint tenants.

Please refer to *Joint property ownership* and practice guide *24: private trusts of land* for further guidance. These are both available on the GOV.UK website.

9   The transferor transfers with

☒   full title guarantee

☐   limited title guarantee

10   Declaration of trust. The transferee is more than one person and

☒   they are to hold the property on trust for themselves as joint tenants ❹

☐   they are to hold the property on trust for themselves as tenants in common in equal shares

☐   they are to hold the property on trust:

Insert here any required or permitted statement, certificate or application and any agreed covenants, declarations and so on.

11   Additional provisions
 ❺

The transferor must execute this transfer as a deed using the space opposite. If there is more than one transferor, all must execute. Forms of execution are given in Schedule 9 to the Land Registration Rules 2003. If the transfer contains transferee's covenants or declarations or contains an application by the transferee (such as for a restriction), it must also be executed by the transferee.

12   Execution

 Signed as a Deed by FS Housing Corporation ❻

If there is more than one transferee and panel 10 has been completed, each transferee must also execute this transfer to comply with the requirements in section 53(1)(b) of the Law of Property Act 1925 relating to the declaration of a trust of land. Please refer to *Joint property ownership* and practice guide *24: private trusts of land* for further guidance.

Examples of the correct form of execution are set out in practice guide 8: execution of deeds. Execution as a deed usually means that a witness must also sign, and add their name and address.

Remember to date this deed in panel 3.

⑦

WARNING
If you dishonestly enter information or make a statement that you know is, or might be, untrue or misleading, and intend by doing so to make a gain for yourself or another person, or to cause loss or the risk of loss to another person, you may commit the offence of fraud under section 1 of the Fraud Act 2006, the maximum penalty for which is 10 years' imprisonment or an unlimited fine, or both.

Failure to complete this form with proper care may result in a loss of protection under the Land Registration Act 2002 if, as a result, a mistake is made in the register.

Under section 66 of the Land Registration Act 2002 most documents (including this form) kept by the registrar relating to an application to the registrar or referred to in the register are open to public inspection and copying. If you believe a document contains prejudicial information, you may apply for that part of the document to be made exempt using Form EX1, under rule 136 of the Land Registration Rules 2003.

© Crown copyright (ref: LR/HO) 08/23

## COMMENTARY

① The transfer is drafted poorly. Panel 5 does not include the correct full names from the contract. This could create future problems as there could be more than one V Khatri living at this address.

② In panel 6, the transfer refers to the address as being the address of the property that the clients are buying. This could cause significant problems in the future. If the tenant or someone else tried to fraudulently register something against the client's title, the client may not receive Land Registry correspondence as it would be going to the address that the tenant is residing in. This could result in a claim being made against the firm for professional misconduct.

③ Panel 8 has been completed incorrectly. The full purchase price should be stated, rather than the amount left to complete the transaction. This enables the Land Registry to ensure that the correct Stamp Duty Land Tax (SDLT) has been paid and there has been no tax avoidance.

④ Panel 10 does not comply with the clients' instructions. As it currently stands, if one of the clients were to die, the other would own the property wholly, despite the clients' clear instructions to be tenants in common. The property would pass automatically upon the death of one to the remaining joint tenant via survivorship, and irrespective of the clients' wishes, if they were to have a will. This could potentially result in a professional negligence claim being brought against the firm.

⑤ Panel 11 does not include an indemnity covenant. However, the title is clear that there is one. Although less of an issue when acting on behalf of a buyer, this is poor practice. The seller could technically end up being responsible for a breach of covenant that they no longer have any control over.

⑥ The final panel is problematic as it does not validly convey the legal title to the new owners. Transfers are legal documents that need to be correctly executed for the new owners to be registered with the Land Registry. Without this, there is potential for the sellers to have taken the completion monies and still legally own the property. In addition, as the seller is a company, either two directors or a director and company secretary should sign on behalf of the company.

⑦ In terms of the clients being a party to sign, as there should be an indemnity covenant in panel 11 there should also be an execution clause for the clients in panel 12. It is not always necessary for a buyer to sign a transfer; it is only if there is an indemnity covenant or declaration of some sort.

## Does this answer meet the threshold?

When assessing the second transfer against the SQE2 legal drafting assessment criteria, it is unlikely that this transfer would meet the threshold standard for SQE2 legal drafting. It will not be a valid legal deed and therefore the Land Registry will not register the new legal owners. This could result in a professional negligence claim being made against the firm.

## ■ KEY POINT CHECKLIST

This chapter has covered the following key knowledge points:
- The SQE2 assessment criteria for legal drafting and how to apply them in the context of property practice.
- A suggested structure for approaching an SQE2 legal drafting assessment question.
- Examples of contracts and transfers that are either likely or unlikely to meet the threshold standard, with full commentary on their strengths and weaknesses.

## ■ SUMMARY AND REFLECTION

To succeed in the SQE2 legal drafting assessment, you will need to carefully read all of the information provided in the supporting documents before beginning to draft the contract or transfer.

Remember that names will need to marry up with the information that you have already been provided with, and you will be given all of the information needed to draft a competent legal contract and transfer.

Make sure you practise drafting execution panels in a correct legal manner to ensure the validity of the conveyance of the legal estate to your clients. If you do not follow the correct requirements, the transfer would be invalid, and you will be penalised for this in the assessment.

Now take the time to reflect and consider what you might still need to work on, and whether you feel completely confident in your legal drafting skills in the context of property practice.

# Final words

We hope that the guidance and examples contained in this book have helped to put into context how to use your practice skills to ensure you reach the SQE2 grading criteria. Remember, above all, that this is an assessment, and the examiner needs to see evidence that you have met the criteria in order for you to pass the threshold. Always keep this in the back of your mind when taking your SQE2 assessments.

While this book is designed to aid your learning and provide helpful tips on how to pass your SQE2 assessments, it is no substitute for practice. All skills are improved with repetition and refining your technique, and legal skills are no exception to this rule. Take any opportunity you can to write letters, draft legal documents and practise your interviewing and advocacy skills. Reflect carefully on your performance after each exercise:
- What could you have done better?
- Did you meet all of the grading criteria applicable to that particular skill?
- Do you need to fill any gaps in your legal knowledge?

Constant practice and self-reflection are the keys to success.

Finally, the team at *Revise SQE* wish you the best of luck in your SQE2 assessments!

# Appendix

## PERFORMANCE INDICATORS FOR SQE2
## CASE AND MATTER ANALYSIS ASSESSMENT CRITERIA

| Skills | Indicators demonstrating competence | Indicators that do not demonstrate competence |
|---|---|---|
| Identify relevant facts | • The candidate selects facts that are important in ensuring the client's needs/objectives are met, or are relevant to the legal analysis, from the documentation provided | • The candidate refers to all facts from the documentation, regardless of whether or not they are important in meeting the client's objectives or relevant to their legal analysis<br><br>• The candidate refers only to irrelevant facts<br><br>• The candidate does not refer to sufficient relevant facts to support the legal analysis |
| Provide client-focused advice (ie advice that demonstrates an understanding of the problem from the client's point of view and what the client wants to achieve, not just from a legal perspective) | • The candidate demonstrates an understanding of the client's problem from the client's perspective<br><br>• The candidate addresses the client's legal problem, any relevant commercial considerations and/or the client's personal circumstances, priorities, objectives and constraints | • The candidate does not approach or appreciate the client's problem from the client's perspective<br><br>• The candidate does not focus on the issues identified by the client |
| Use clear, precise, concise and acceptable language | • The reader understands the candidate's use of language and clarity of expression<br><br>• The candidate avoids unnecessary technical terms/legal jargon | • The reader struggles to understand the candidate's use of language; the answer lacks clarity and/or is poorly expressed<br><br>• The reader's understanding is adversely affected by the density, length or brevity of the answer<br><br>• The candidate uses unnecessary technical terms/legal jargon |

| Law | Indicators demonstrating competence | Indicators that do not demonstrate competence |
|---|---|---|
| Apply the law correctly to the client's situation | • The candidate identifies the relevant fundamental legal principles in accordance with the SQE2 assessment specification and applies them correctly to the facts of the client's case | • The candidate does not identify and correctly apply the relevant legal principles to the facts of the client's case<br><br>• The candidate does not apply the relevant legal principles in a way that addresses the client's needs and concerns |
| Apply the law comprehensively to the client's situation, identifying any ethical and professional conduct issues and exercising judgement to resolve them honestly and with integrity | • The candidate's legal analysis is sufficiently detailed in the context of the client's case, eg assessing information to identify key issues and risks; reaching reasonable conclusions supported by relevant evidence<br><br>• Where relevant, the candidate recognises ethical issues and exercises effective judgement in addressing them in accordance with the SRA Principles and rules of professional conduct | • The candidate's legal analysis is not sufficiently detailed in the context of the client's case, eg the candidate demonstrates little or no understanding of the key issues and risks; fails to apply the law to the facts to reach reasonable conclusions<br><br>• The candidate does not recognise ethical issues or exercise effective judgement in addressing them in accordance with the SRA Principles and rules of professional conduct |

## PERFORMANCE INDICATORS FOR SQE2 LEGAL RESEARCH ASSESSMENT CRITERIA

| Skills | Indicators demonstrating competence | Indicators that do not demonstrate competence |
|---|---|---|
| Identify and use relevant sources and information | • The candidate selects relevant information about the legal issue, or the client's problem, from the primary and/or secondary sources provided, eg<br><br>  o the candidate identifies relevant legislation/cases and/or legal explanations/commentary in a practitioner's text, or legal encyclopaedia<br><br>  o the candidate extracts relevant material, such as particular provision(s) from a statute, or legal rule(s) from the Civil Procedure Rules<br><br>• The candidate uses their findings to substantiate/support their answer to the question(s) asked | • The candidate selects only irrelevant information from the primary and/or secondary sources provided<br><br>• The candidate selects insufficient relevant information from the primary and/or secondary sources provided<br><br>• The candidate is unable to distinguish between information that is relevant to the legal issue or the client's problem, and information that is irrelevant, eg the candidate's answer contains information drawn from all sources regardless of relevance, or from a number of irrelevant sources<br><br>• The candidate does not use their findings to substantiate/support the answer to the question(s) asked |
| Provide advice that is client-focused and addresses the client's problem | • The candidate demonstrates an understanding of the client's problem from the client's perspective, eg the candidate addresses the client's legal problem, any relevant commercial considerations and/or the client's priorities, objectives and constraints | • The candidate does not understand the problem from the client's perspective, eg they focus on irrelevant issues/provide advice that does not take into account the client's priorities, objectives or constraints, or is inappropriate for the client's situation |
| Use clear, precise, concise and acceptable language | • The candidate uses understandable and simple language to convey facts and information effectively<br><br>• The candidate uses correct legal terminology where necessary | • The reader struggles to understand the candidate's use of language; the answer lacks clarity and/or is poorly expressed<br><br>• The reader's understanding is adversely affected by the density or brevity of the answer<br><br>• The candidate uses unnecessary or confusing technical terms/legal jargon |

| Law | Indicators demonstrating competence | Indicators that do not demonstrate competence |
|---|---|---|
| **Apply the law correctly to the client's situation** | • The candidate identifies the relevant legal principles and applies them correctly to the facts of the client's case | • The candidate does not identify and apply the correct legal principles to the facts of the client's case<br><br>• The candidate identifies the correct legal principles but misapplies them to the client's case |
| **Apply the law comprehensively to the client's situation, identifying any ethical and professional conduct issues and exercising judgement to resolve them honestly and with integrity** | • The candidate's legal analysis is sufficiently detailed in the context of the facts of the case, eg the candidate draws on multiple sources of information to address the legal issue/client's problem effectively<br><br>• Where relevant, the candidate recognises ethical issues and exercises effective judgement in addressing them in accordance with the SRA Principles and rules of professional conduct | • The candidate's legal analysis is not sufficiently detailed in the context of the facts of the client's case<br><br>• The candidate does not recognise ethical issues or exercise effective judgement in addressing them in accordance with the SRA Principles and rules of professional conduct |

# PERFORMANCE INDICATORS FOR SQE2 LEGAL WRITING ASSESSMENT CRITERIA

| Skills | Indicators demonstrating competence | Indicators that do not demonstrate competence |
|---|---|---|
| Include relevant facts | • The candidate refers to and/or addresses the salient facts provided in their instructions. Salient facts could include facts that are important in ensuring the client's needs/objectives are met, or relevant to legal advice | • The candidate includes many facts in their answer that have no bearing on their legal advice |
| Use a logical structure | • The candidate's presentation of information is well organised, set out clearly and easy to follow<br>• The reader is able to understand the candidate's answer without difficulty | • The candidate's presentation of information is confused and rambling<br>• The reader is unable to follow or understand the candidate's answer |
| Advice/content is client- and recipient-focused | • The candidate demonstrates an understanding of the client's circumstances including their needs, objectives and priorities<br>• The candidate, where relevant and appropriate, explores options and advises on strategies and solutions<br>• The candidate takes into account who the client is; recognises the key issues in the case and considers any risks<br>• Where appropriate, the candidate imparts any difficult or unwelcome news clearly and sensitively | • The candidate does not understand the client's perspective, eg they focus on irrelevant issues/provide extraneous advice/fail to advise on relevant options, strategies and solutions<br>• The candidate fails to take into account who the client is and does not recognise the key issues in the case or consider any risks<br>• The candidate lacks empathy or sensitivity if imparting difficult or unwelcome news |
| Use clear, precise, concise and acceptable language that is appropriate to the recipient | • The reader understands the candidate's use of language and clarity of expression<br>• The candidate's language is appropriate to the recipient and the situation<br>• The candidate avoids unnecessary technical terms/legal jargon<br>• The candidate uses formalities appropriate to the context and purpose of the communication | • The reader struggles to understand the candidate's use of language; the answer lacks clarity and/or is poorly expressed<br>• The reader's understanding is adversely affected by the density or brevity of the answer<br>• The candidate uses language that is not appropriate to the recipient and/or the situation, eg the candidate adopts an essay-style approach<br>• The candidate uses unnecessary or confusing technical terms/legal jargon |

| Law | Indicators demonstrating competence | Indicators that do not demonstrate competence |
|---|---|---|
| Apply the law correctly to the client's situation | • The candidate identifies the correct legal principles and applies them correctly to the facts of the case | • The candidate does not identify the correct legal principles<br><br>• The candidate does not apply the legal principles correctly to the client's situation |
| Apply the law comprehensively to the client's situation, identifying any ethical and professional conduct issues and exercising judgement to resolve them honestly and with integrity | • The candidate's writing is of sufficient detail in the context of the client's situation and the relevant factual and legal issues<br><br>• Where relevant, the candidate recognises ethical issues and exercises effective judgement in addressing them in accordance with the SRA Principles and rules of professional conduct | • The candidate's writing is not sufficiently detailed in the context of the client's situation and the relevant factual and legal issues<br><br>• The candidate does not recognise ethical issues or exercise effective judgement in addressing them in accordance with the SRA Principles and rules of professional conduct |

# PERFORMANCE INDICATORS FOR SQE2 LEGAL DRAFTING ASSESSMENT CRITERIA

| Skills | Indicators demonstrating competence | Indicators that do not demonstrate competence |
|---|---|---|
| Use clear, precise, concise and acceptable language | • The candidate uses understandable and simple language to convey facts and information effectively<br><br>• The candidate uses words and phrases that are suitably formal for the document being drafted<br><br>• The candidate uses correct legal terminology where necessary<br><br>• The document uses as few words as possible without compromising the quality of the answer | • The candidate's answer is consistently wordy, repetitive or confusing and cannot be easily understood<br><br>• The meaning of the document cannot be ascertained because it contains few words<br><br>• The candidate uses inappropriate language, eg the language is too informal or casual<br><br>• The candidate uses unnecessary technical terms/ legal jargon throughout |
| Structure the document appropriately and logically | • The candidate presents facts and information in a methodical way, eg the focus, flow and direction of each paragraph is clear and appropriate signposts are used to guide the reader through the document<br><br>• The way in which the candidate sets out the contents of the document achieve its purpose | • The candidate's arrangement of facts or information is disjointed or confusing, eg the paragraphing or sequencing of information is illogical<br><br>• The way in which the candidate sets out the contents of the document does not achieve its purpose |
| Law | Indicators demonstrating competence | Indicators that do not demonstrate competence |
| Draft a document that is legally correct | • The candidate identifies the correct legal principles in accordance with the SQE2 assessment specification and applies them correctly in their drafting<br><br>• The candidate's drafting is legally effective, eg the document contains all key information or the names of relevant parties | • The candidate does not identify the correct legal principles<br><br>• The candidate does not apply the legal principles correctly in their drafting<br><br>• The candidate's drafting is not legally effective |
| Draft a document that is legally comprehensive, identifying any ethical and professional conduct issues and exercising judgement to resolve them honestly and with integrity | • The candidate's drafting is sufficiently detailed in the context of the client's situation and the relevant factual and legal issues<br><br>• Where relevant, the candidate recognises ethical issues and exercises effective judgement in addressing them in accordance with the SRA Principles and rules of professional conduct | • The candidate's drafting is not sufficiently detailed in the context of the client's situation and the relevant factual and legal issues<br><br>• The candidate does not recognise ethical issues or exercise effective judgement in addressing them in accordance with the SRA Principles and rules of professional conduct |

www.ingramcontent.com/pod-product-compliance
Lightning Source LLC
Chambersburg PA
CBHW082103210326
41599CB00033B/6564